W9-AOG-898

Desire and Death
In the Spanish
Sentimental Romance

# Desire and Death in the
# Spanish Sentimental Romance
# (1440-1550)

*by*

Patricia E. Grieve

*Williams College and Columbia University*

## Juan de la Cuesta
Newark, Delaware

Copyright © 1987 by Juan de la Cuesta—Hispanic Monographs
270 Indian Road
Newark, Delaware 19711

MANUFACTURED IN THE UNITED STATES OF AMERICA

The pH of the paper this book is printed on is 7.00.

ISBN: 0-936388-22-6
Library of Congress Catalogue Card Number: 84-80096

*For Alan Deyermond*

# Contents

# List of Abbreviations

# Acknowledgments

THIS BOOK IS A revised version of my doctoral dissertation. Since that time, I have new colleagues to thank for their support and encouragement, and two previous debts continue to require acknowledgment.

Williams College, where I was Visiting Assistant Professor from 1982-84, and where I completed my dissertation in 1983, generously provided funds towards the publication of this book. I am grateful to Columbia University for their support for the same purpose.

I am particularly grateful to E. Michael Gerli for his invaluable advice on this manuscript and to my editor, Thomas Lathrop, for his encouragement in this project.

My deepest debt of gratitude continues to be to my thesis director, Alan Deyermond, of Westfield College, University of London. I will always be grateful that his visiting professorship at Princeton coincided with the years of my doctoral program. His classes were a joy, his encouragement unwavering. In the prologue to *Arnalte y Lucenda*, Diego de San Pedro begged his readers, "que la burla sea secreta, y el favor público." Professor Deyermond's criticism of my work has ranged from gentle to harsh—and always justifiably so. But his support of his students goes above and beyond the call of duty and they, unlike the apprehensive San Pedro, need never expect anything but encouragement and honest criticism. In spite of the distance between New York and London, the crackling telephone lines and erratic mail delivery, Professor Deyermond has continued to demonstrate great interest in my publications and my talks at conferences. Therefore, it is indeed with my deepest gratitude that I dedicate this study to my teacher, greatest critic, staunchest supporter, and friend—Alan Deyermond.

P.E.G.
*Columbia University*

Digo muy más el omne que toda criatura:
todas a tiempo cierto se juntan, con natura;
el omne de mal seso, todo tiempo, sin mesura,
cada que puede quier'. fazer esta locura.

El fuego siempre quiere estar en la ceniza,
comoquier que más arde quanto más se atiza;
el omne quando peca bien vee que desliza,
más no se parte ende, ca natura lo enriza.[1]

## INTRODUCTION

JUAN RUIZ RECOUNTED MANY tales of seduction and attempted seduction in the fourteenth-century *Libro de buen amor*. Unfortunately for the world's lovers, one of the book's messages is startlingly clear: sexual desire, although a natural human instinct, is a form of madness. In spite of the repeated poetic testimony to love as an ennobling force, given by writers from Provençal troubadours to contemporary songwriters, voices of dissent have been heard throughout the centuries. Writers were not alone in their dissenting opinions: "There is an area of medieval culture in which philosophy, literature, and medicine are intimately intertwined. Official doctrine and science (specifically, medicine) agreed in condemning love as a sort of disease or madness."[2]

Nowhere is love's conflictive nature more evident than in fifteenth-century Spain. The courtly love tradition was revitalized in Spain, as Roger Boase shows us, as a response to changes occurring in

---

[1] Juan Ruiz, *Libro de buen amor*, ed., and trans. by Raymond S. Willis (Princeton: University Press, 1972), stanzas 74-75, p. 31.

[2] Aldo D. Scaglione, *Nature and Love in the Late Middle Ages* (Berkeley: University of California Press, 1963), p. 60. For a discussion of love as an illness, see Keith Whinnom's introduction to San Pedro's *Obras completas*, II: *Cárcel de Amor*, Clásicos Castalia, 39 (Madrid: Castalia, 1971), pp. 13-15. For a study of the ancestry of the idea of love-as-illness, see John Livingston Lowes, "The Loveres' Maladye of Heroes," *MP*, 11 (1913-14), 491-546 and Bruno Nardi, "L'amore e i medici medievali" in *Studi in onore Angelo Monteverdi* (Modena: 1959), pp. 517-42.

all of Europe which threatened to prove the uselessness of the aristocracy:

> It was my general conclusion that this cultural phenomenon [the revival of troubadour poetry] was a form of archaism, that is to say, a response by the dominant minority to the disintegration of medieval values and institutions.
>
> In the late Middle Ages many European countries were dominated, both politically and culturally, by an aristocracy which was in danger of becoming professionally redundant as a result of its inability to adapt to sudden changes in the nature of society, chief of which were the absence of chivalry in the methods and motives of mechanised warfare, the growth of centralised bureaucracy and the development of a non-seignorial economy.... This social group looked back with nostalgia to a largely imaginary chivalric age, and rejected as subversive and heretical any social concepts which denied the immutable providential character of the status quo. The Provençal ideal of *fin'amors* answered the needs of this dominant minority because, being based on the feudal principles of fealty and subservience, it inculcated a respect for status and the existing hierarchy and was a means of evading unpleasant social and political realities.[3]

The whole concept of courtly love is problematic, and it is not my intent to address the issue of definition and rules: that has been done recently by others.[4] What I mean, however, is that body of poetry and

---

[3] *The Troubadour Revival: A Study of Social Change and Traditionalism in Late Medieval Spain* (London: Routledge and Kegan Paul, 1978), pp. 151-52. See also Antony van Beysterveldt, *Amadís-Esplandián-Calisto: Historia de un linaje adulterado* (Madrid: José Porrúa Turanzas, 1982).

[4] As everyone is aware by now "amour courtois" is a term originated by the nineteenth-century critic, Gaston Paris. The term itself has fallen into disrepute recently because it seems to be misleading. Critics felt that there was a codified system called "amour courtois" which consisted of rigid rules. As it became apparent through literary analysis that the exceptions to these rules compiled by critics became too numerous to count, the term was dismissed as useless. It remains true, however, that there were courtly love affairs recorded in literature which embodied some, but not always all, of the characteristics most readily associated with courtly love. In other words, the debate over what to call it does not negate the phenomenon itself. A recent study by Roger Boase, *The Origin and Meaning of Courtly Love: A Critical Study of European Scholarship* (Manchester: University Press, 1977), is a sound examination of the phenomenon as it appeared in different countries and centuries, as well as a history of the criticism of courtly love.

of prose fiction which flourished in medieval courts, was aristocratic in origin and was intended for a similarly aristocratic audience. A recurrent feature of this literature is the "belle dame sans merci." Even in the best of circumstances, as when a woman is praised most highly for her beauty, nobility, and virtue, she causes pain, despair, death as a result of the love she inspires in the male lover. The glories of love are matched by the despair inherent in its condition. Paradoxically, it is when one is most in love that the pain is greatest. The explanation comes from the correlative courtly notion that the beloved is unattainable. Women were clearly in an untenable position: the unattainable woman is the most virtuous, a favorable quality one would think, but she is constantly railed against by her poet/lover for her cruelty in withholding her favors.

This is not to say that women authors and women's perspectives were not represented in the love lyric, nor that the male poets describe only those relationships of unrequited love.[5] This example, from one of Juan de Mena's minor poems, indicates that the man's passion is reciprocated by the woman, or, at least, implies some kind of physical involvement:

> Donde yago en esta cama
> la mayor pena de mí
> es pensar quando partí
> de entre braços de mi dama.[6]

More often than not, however, women were portrayed in unflattering ways. In fact, when they were not railing against the cruelty of the lady who withheld her favors, men often cited women's lustful nature.[7] This paradoxical view of woman as the "belle dame sans

---

[5] For a study of some women poets of the Middle Ages, see, for example, Meg Bogin, *The Women Troubadours* (New York: Paddington Press, 1976) and Jack Lindsay, *The Troubadours and Their World of the twelfth and Thirteenth Centuries* (London: Frederick Muller, 1976), especially "Arabic Influences," pp. 154-66, "Arnaut Daniel and other Troubadours including Women," pp. 167-89, and "Folksongs and Popular Bases," pp. 190-202.

[6] *Obra lírica*, ed. Miguel Angel Pérez Priego (Madrid: Alhambra, 1979), p. 67.

[7] In *The Troubadours and Their World*, Lindsay says: "The tales about women ready and even zealous to commit adultery are not all fiction or antifeminist convention. The twelfth and even more the thirteenth century saw a widespread revolt of women against the standards imposed on them by the men, against the unequal rule in marriage, against the endless insults from the church," p. 90.

merci" and the creature of an insatiable sexual appetite was reinforced in the literature of vituperative nature, the misogynist treatises such as Martínez de Toledo's *Corbacho* and the prose and poetry of Pere Toroellas.[8]

The poets of fifteenth-century Spain celebrated courtly love affairs with an amazing quantity of poetry, much of which we have today in the surviving collections of poetry, called *cancioneros*. In the second half of the fifteenth century, love was treated by several authors in a different way, best described as a transformation of *cancionero* love lyric to longer works, either a combination of prose and poetry or entirely in prose, which frequently incorporated the misogynists' view of women. The *cancionero* love poetry is often a lamentation; these other works, often called sentimental romances,[9] tell us what led up to the lamentation and, in the works to be examined in this study, that which followed the lamentation. I mean this not in a literal sense but in a metaphorical one: the sentimental romances rarely contain the same poems as the *cancionero*, but rather the same type of poetic metaphors and themes. The poetic lamentations, although often viewed as an outpouring of truthful emotion on the part of the author, are at best only partial truths since they capture only one moment in time and do not tell the whole story. In addition, they are designed to engage the sympathies of the listener by presenting just one person's point of view. Since almost all the *cancionero* poets were men—Florencia Pinar being the only woman represented by several extant poems[10]—the point of view of half the members of the amorous duos was sadly lacking.

[8] On the ancestry of this misogynist writing in Spain, see Christine J. Whitbourn, *The "Arcipreste de Talavera" and the Literature of Love*, Occasional Papers in Modern Languages, 7 (Hull: University, 1970) and Jacob Ornstein, "La misoginia y el profeminismo en la literatura castellana," *RFH*, 3 (1941), 219-32. On the general European tradition, see Francis Lee Utley, *The Crooked Rib: An Analytical Index to the Argument about Women in English and Scots Literature to the End of the Year 1568* (Columbus: The Ohio State University, 1944) and Katharine M. Rogers, *The Troublesome Helpmate: A History of Misogyny in Literature* (Seattle: University of Washington Press, 1966).

[9] Menéndez y Pelayo and others have referred to the works as "novelas sentimentales" but this is misleading since they are rightly called not novels, but romances.

[10] Florencia Pinar's works can be found in the *Cancionero general*; in this and other *cancioneros* some poems are anonymous so the possibility exists that there are other female *cancionero* poets. There are, however, some fragments of poems by women.

It would be an overstatement to say that, happily, the sentimental romances remedied this neglect because here, too, the writers were male, but they do provide a broader perspective. In being given the whole story we witness a variety of culprits for unhappy love affairs from the actions of cruel fathers to those of jealous rivals to love itself, when seen as a dynamic force. Women do not always fare well in these texts, either in how they are portrayed or in what befalls them, but at least love is seen in a broader context than it appears in the *cancioneros*.

*Siervo libre de amor*, c. 1440, which contains the tale *Estoria de dos amadores*, has long been recognized as the prototype of the sentimental romances of the second half of the fifteenth century and the first half of the sixteenth. The exact degree of influence of *Siervo libre* on the later works is difficult to pinpoint and is widely debated.[11] The other point of contention is the sources of *Siervo libre* itself: the major contenders are Boccaccio's *Elegia di Madonna Fiammetta* and Aeneas Sylvius Piccolomini's *Historia de duobus amantibus*.[12]

To decide what constitutes a sentimental romance has proven to be a thorny problem for critics. When critics have listed the sentimental romances, either in histories of literature or in books on the genre, the lists vary. The sentimental romances employ many of the same elements, but no work contains all the elements which have been identified as pertaining to the genre, such as intermediaries, secret messages, autobiographical narrative, violence, the use of letters, the use of verse and, above all, the insistence upon love as a venture destined for unhappiness. Since the works differ greatly from each other, a theory of the genre has eluded critics, although some theories have been suggested. That there are differences between the works explains why there are variants in the critics' lists: each one selects his own list of important elements so that the aberrations can

---

[11] *Siervo libre* is the subject of Chapter I of this study. Bibliography on the points of source and influence is given there.

[12] A recent study suggests that too much emphasis has been placed on the role of these two Italian works in the evolution of the sentimental romance. See Olga Tudoricǎ Impey, "Ovid, Alfonso X, and Juan Rodríguez del Padrón: Two Castilian Translations of the *Heroides* and the Beginnings of Spanish Sentimental Prose," *BHS*, 57 (1980), 283-97. For recent views on the influence of Dante on Rodríguez del Padrón, see Gregory Peter Andrachuk, "A Further Look at Italian Influence in the *Siervo libre de amor*," *JHP*, 6 (1981-82), 45-56 and Marina Scordilis Brownlee, "The Generic Status of the *Siervo libre de amor*: Rodríguez del Padrón's Reworking of Dante," *PoT*, 5, no. 3 (1984), 629-43.

be eliminated. As for lengthier treatments of the sentimental romances, the most notable ones are the works of Dinko Cvitanovič and Armando Durán.[13]

The purpose of this study is to examine some sentimental romances separately and, ultimately, to learn in what way they form a genre. Durán's attempt, while interesting, failed by being too reductive and too selective in the works examined—his study did not capture the essence of each romance. On the other hand, I did not want my own study to be merely a collection of diverse essays, so it was necessary to find a common thread to follow while permitting the uniqueness of each work to come through.

As a point of departure, the sentimental romances are divided into two general categories: frustrated love and violent love. Frustrated love refers to those texts which end either in the imprisonment of the lovers, such as Urrea's *Penitençia de amor*, or result in being the catalogue of notable and notorious women, such as the Constable of Portugal's *Sátira de la felice e infelice vida* and Luis de Lucena's *Repetiçión de amores*, or are more like theoretical treatises on love, such as *Cuestión de amor*, the anonymous work written and published in Naples in 1501.

The texts of frustrated love seem to follow the normal pattern of the courtly love process. They are, often, simply narrative versions of *cancionero* poetry. This is not to say that they are not done well: some are masterful handlings of classical examples of frustrated, tragic love, and some, such as *Penitençia de amor*, are interesting tales. As mentioned earlier, courtly love is by nature contradictory in its rules of passion, and is not destined to have a happy ending: that is neither expected nor possible.

Of course the problem does not end there. The texts of frustrated love themselves divide into two general groups: those in which the

---

[13] Dinko Cvitanovič's work, *La novela sentimental española* (Madrid: Editorial Prensa Española, 1973), attempts a synthesis of some of the sentimental romances' more common elements. He discusses their generic unity throughout his study, but especially in the chapter "El problema de la unidad," pp. 299-313. Armando Durán's study, *Estructura y técnicas de la novela sentimental y caballeresca* (Madrid: Gredos, 1973), reduces the structure of the sentimental romances to main events in order to demonstrate their dependence on either *Elegia di Madonna Fiammetta* or *Historia de duobus amantibus*. For a thorough bibliography on the sentimental romances, see Keith Whinnom, *The Spanish Sentimental Romance 1440-1550: A Critical Bibliography*, Research Bibliographies and Checklists, 41 (London: Grant and Cutler, 1983).

lament or outcry against love and/or women is stated at the outset, and those in which the reader sees clearly that the unhappy affair is the fault not of the lovers but of some other character. We could also say, by resorting to some generalizations, that the sentimental romances of frustrated love follow the model of the frame story of *Siervo libre de amor*: an autobiographical account of an unsuccessful affair. Those romances which follow the general style of *Siervo libre's* intercalated story, *Estoria de dos amadores*—third-person narration involving love triangles—are more likely to be the romances of violent love.

But the texts of violent love do not lend themselves quite so neatly to categorization. Therein lies the problem, as stated earlier, of the tension between the critics' tendency to resort to arbitrary selection of criteria for sentimental romances and the texts' stubborn resistance to such generalizations. Simply stated, the texts of violent love are more inventive and more complex than those of frustrated love. The focus, in each text, will be on the nature of the violence which comes about by the cause-and-effect process of desire. In *Estoria de dos amadores*, for example, we see evidence of this process but, as the analysis will show, no real blame can be attached to the protagonists themselves: it is the father's evil quest which brings about the heroine's death and, indirectly, his own son's death. In the other texts the violence results from desire, and it takes particular forms: suicide in order to save the other lover differs from suicide resulting from unrequited love. Many violent actions occur in the texts, from torture to murder by fire, sword, mutilation and suicide. Death can be the end result of an infraction of society's norms, the unbridled passion of lovers, an autonomous force called love, or a combination of these. In other words, we see similar results provoked by what can generally be termed desire, but which, in fact, occur in distinctive and distinguishing circumstances.

Juan de Segura's *Processo de cartas de amores* poses a problem similar to that of *Siervo libre de amor* inasmuch as both works have an autobiographical part and one in third-person narration. Segura's work is the story of frustrated love, in which the lady he loves retires to a convent and the lover resigns himself to a life without her. The appended story, *Quexa y aviso de un caballero llamado Luzindaro contra amor y una dama y sus casos*, has never been analyzed; when it has been mentioned, it is usually to say that the analysis of *Processo de cartas* is completely independent of this tale. Yet it is clearly the intention of the author, as we shall see, that the meaning, or value, of his work lies in the consideration of the two parts of the work, not simply in the first part, *Processo de cartas*. Therefore, *Processo de cartas* will be treated as will *Siervo libre*: the analysis will deal with the two tales of death-- *Estoria de dos amadores* and *Luzindaro y Medusina (Quexa y aviso)*--but always with the intention of resolving the connection of the autobiographical part of the works with these tales.

Three chapters are devoted to the two major writers of sentimental romances, Diego de San Pedro (*Tractado de amores de Arnalte y Lucenda* and *Cárcel de Amor*) and Juan de Flores (*Grisel y Mirabella* and *Grimalte y Gradissa*). *Cárcel de Amor* and *Arnalte y Lucenda* present slightly different cases from the others since neither text involves the violent death of one or both lovers, although in *Cárcel* the male lover commits suicide through starvation. Nevertheless, there is violence in the text resulting from the impetus of desire.

In the last chapter, brief consideration will be given to a work which does not receive a separate chapter, *Triste deleytaçión*, but which could be seen as a bridge between the work of Rodríguez del Padrón, on the one hand, and the romances of San Pedro and Flores, on the other.

It is the intent of this study, then, to analyze six works—the first sentimental romance, the last one, and the four written by San Pedro and Flores—always following the theme of desire and resultant death, and then to provide a suggestion for how we can see these works as a subgenre of the larger sentimental one. The final chapter will elaborate the theme of love and death and the interplay of literature and life in these texts and will suggest a structural and thematic framework within which to view the romances of violent love.

This is by no means an exhaustive study: much research remains to be done on all the romances and, in particular, on the lesser-known ones. For example, the relationship of chivalric literature in Spain to the sentimental romances offers one area of great potential; links between the romances and the material of the *cancioneros* and *romanceros* remain unclear. Moreover, these romances could be fruitfully studied as precursors to much of late sixteenth and seventeenth-century prose fiction. What is clear, however, is the richness of the texts and the certain knowledge that they embody many strains of literary development—from within Spain and without—and that their study continues to enhance our understanding of a complex period of Spanish letters.

# Juan Rodríguez del Padrón's
## *Siervo libre de amor*
## and *Estoria de dos amadores:*
# From Loyalty to Legend

"Amores me dieron corona de amores
Porque mi nonbre por más bocas ande."
MACÍAS, in *Laberinto de Fortuna*, stanza 106

UAN RODRÍGUEZ DEL PADRÓN fancied himself a troubadour and a lover, and allied himself with the expressed desires and noble deeds of courtiers from days gone by—Macías, Tristan and now, Ardanlier, from *Estoria de dos amadores*, the intercalated story in *Siervo libre de amor*.[1] A necessary step for the author was to infuse his story of Ardanlier and Liessa with images and reminiscences of heroines and heroes both historical and literary. A reworking of the miracle of the Virgin of Liesse, some similarities with Arthurian material and the Tristan and Iseult legend in particular, an association with the maligned and murdered Dona Inês de Castro and allusion to Santiago and San Juan, all work together to elevate the Spanish legend, newly created by Rodríguez del Padrón, to the regard

---

[1] For a discussion of the literary relationship of Macías to Rodríguez del Padrón, see Carlos Martínez-Barbeito, *Macías el enamorado y Juan Rodríguez del Padrón*, Biblioteca de Galicia, 4 (Santiago de Compostela: Sociedad de Bibliófilos Gallegos, 1951).

accorded to lovers' histories from other lands and to establish a religion of love and pilgrimages of love.[2]

Rodríguez del Padrón championed two causes for Spanish letters in one work. First, by associating Ardanlier and Liessa with traditional star-crossed lovers who were revered and celebrated in French and Latin works, he created for Spain, and for Galicia in particular, its own pair of lovers who would, no doubt, inspire love pilgrimages. No longer need the Spanish courtiers rely on Tristan and Iseult, Dido, Paris, and countless others. Galicia now could be proud of its own indigenous legend. Simply to see Galicia as a new center of courtly love, in a real sense, as Gilderman does, is to miss the highly conscious literary efforts of the author.[3] Second, by resolving the ambiguities of the frame story, through sophisticated narrative techniques linking it to *EDA*, Rodríguez del Padrón ennobles his own love affair on a personal level and a literary one. He creates a prose form out of contemporary courtly experience. It does not matter what is the outcome of the experience. What matters is the dual legitimization of a Spanish love tale and a contemporary narrative form of a love story. It is the same impulse that caused Mena's comment in *Laberinto de Fortuna* that Spain's heroes go unsung because, unlike other cultures, she has no poets.[4]

*Siervo libre de amor* has not lacked recent criticism. Because it is

---

[2] Marina Scordilis Brownlee, "The Generic Status of the *Siervo libre de amor*: Rodríguez del Padrón's Reworking of Dante," *PoT*, 5, no. 3 (1984), 629-43: "... the mausoleum of the two lovers takes on the aspect of the holy shrine, with all the mystique and ceremony which Santiago de Compostela implies... Clearly, what we have here is a pilgrimage of love—not religion—to Santiago," p. 635.

[3] Martin S. Gilderman, *Juan Rodríguez de la Cámara*, TWAS, 423 (Boston: Twayne, 1977), p. 104: "It may be that Juan Rodríguez, spurned by the Castilian court, created a rival center in his home town—an area which spawned not only saints of the Church, but 'saints' of the religion of love—Ardanlier, Macías, and, lastly, Juan Rodríguez himself, as we shall soon see."

[4] Como non creo que fuessen menores
que los africanos los fechos del Çid,
nin que feroçes menos en la lid
entrassen los nuestros que los agenores
las grandes fanzañadas de nuestros mayores,
la mucha costançia de quien los más ama,
yaze en tinieblas dormida su fama,
dañada de olvido por falta de auctores.

(Juan de Mena, *El laberinto de Fortuna o las trescientas*, ed. Jose Manuel Blecua, Clásicos Castellanos, 119 [Madrid: Espasa-Calpe, 1943; rpt. 1968], stanza 4.)

mysterious, allegorical, and ambiguous, the work provokes differing opinions, especially as to the significance of the ending and the overall intent.[5] For the most part, analysis has focused on the allegorical, autobiographical frame story.[6]

The general intent is clear: the author-narrator, Siervo, relates the unhappy experience he suffered by having loved a woman of the court. He indiscreetly confided in a false friend who subsequently informed the beloved. The unnamed beloved denounced Siervo for his indiscretion and ended the relationship. The sections before EDA consist of a prologue (an outline of the work without mentioning EDA), a letter to

---

[5] The problem with the ending is that there is disagreement as to the completeness of the work. Critics are divided over the belief that a third part is missing. Edward J. Dudley sees *Siervo libre de Amor* as a complete work, designed as an allegory of its literary creation, in "Structure and Meaning in the Novel of Juan Rodríguez: *Siervo libre de amor*," Diss., University of Minnesota, 1963, p. 162. Olga Tudoricǎ Impey sees *Siervo libre* as complete, unified through its theme of loyalty, in two articles, "The Literary Emancipation of Juan Rodríguez del Padrón: From the Fictional 'Cartas' to the *Siervo libre de amor*," *Speculum*, 55 (1980), 305-16, and "Ovid, Alfonso X, and Juan Rodríguez del Padrón: Two Castilian Translations of the *Heroides* and the Beginnings of Spanish Sentimental Prose," *BHS*, 57 (1980), 283-97. See also Juan Fernández Jiménez, "*Siervo libre de amor*: ¿novela incompleta?," *Hispanófila*, no. 75 (May 1982), 1-7, "La estructura del *Siervo libre de amor* y la crítica reciente," *CHA*, 388 (1982), 178-90 and Peter Cocozzella, "The Thematic Unity of Juan Rodríguez del Padrón's *Siervo libre de amor*, *Hispania* 64 (1981), 188-98. Beginning with Menéndez y Pelayo, *Orígenes de la novela*, II (Madrid: CSIC, 1943), p. 19, there has been a steady stream of believers in the work's incompleteness, with most of the criticism, both for and against the idea of a missing part, coming after 1970. See also Gregory Peter Andrachuk, "On the Missing Third Part of *Siervo libre de amor*," *HR*, 45 (1977), 171-80, who proposes an interpretation of EDA as a negative *exemplum* for the repudiation of courtly love, and Javier Herrero, "The Allegorical Structure of the *Siervo libre de amor*," *Speculum*, 55 (1980), 751-64, who believes that the third part would have been a strong rejection of the love experience depicted in *Siervo libre*.

[6] The allegorical interpretation of the frame story, along with references to EDA, is discussed by Antonio Prieto in the introduction to Francisco Serrano Puente's edition of *Siervo libre de amor*, Clásicos Castalia, 66 (Madrid: Castalia, 1976); César Hernández Alonso, "*Siervo libre de amor*" de Juan Rodríguez del Padrón (Valladolid: Universidad, 1970); Armando Durán, *Estructura y técnicas de la novela sentimental y caballeresca* (Madrid: Gredos, 1973), pp. 19-24, 32-35, 42-44, 49-52; Dinko Cvitanović, *La novela sentimental española*, El Soto, 21 (Madrid: Editorial Prensa Española, 1973); María Rosa Lida de Malkiel, "Juan Rodríguez del Padrón: Influencia," *NRFH*, 8 (1954), 1-38.

his patron (Gonzalo de Medina), a narration of the brief and unsuccessful love relationship, and the sections entitled "de bien amar y ser amado" and "Solitaria e dolorosa contemplaçion" in which Siervo travels the allegorical paths, "por la escura selua de mis pensamientos."[7]

EDA is not mentioned in the outline of the work, but it is by no means superfluous. Criticism of EDA has limited itself primarily to literary and historical similarities of character and structure.[8] Edward Dudley, in his unpublished doctoral dissertation, analyzed EDA, but, notwithstanding some perspicacious observations, his focus is incorrect.[9]

The relationship of EDA to the frame story has been touched upon mostly in terms of attempts to identify Siervo with one or more characters in EDA. When they were hard and fast correspondences, they tended to break down as critics presented different evidence in support of one or the other. The relation to EDA of the frame story is strongest when the overall theme of each is compared, the overall structure of EDA is studied, and some concrete links between the two are established.

*"Estoria de dos amadores:" From Loyalty to Legend*

The movement of romance, from disorder to order, is of prime importance in EDA.[10] The author does not settle for a simple happy

[7] *Obras de Juan Rodríguez de la Cámara (o del Padrón)*, Sociedad de Bibliófilos Españoles, 22 (Madrid, 1884), ed. Antonio Paz y Melia, pp. 37-80. This volume also contains Rodríguez del Padrón's translation of Ovid's *Heroides*, called the *Bursario*, pp. 197-313. Unfortunately, the more recent edition of *Siervo libre* from Castalia is unreliable; Paz y Melia is not completely error-free, but is, nonetheless, more reliable than the newer edition.

[8] Gregory Peter Andrachuk, "The Function of the *Estoria de dos amadores* within the *Siervo libre de amor*," *RCEH*, 2 (1977-78), 27-38; D. L. Bastianutti, "La función de la Fortuna en la primera novela sentimental española," *RN*, 14 (1972-73), 394-402; Edward J. Dudley, "Court and Country: The Fusion of Two Images of Love in Juan Rodríguez' *El siervo libre de amor*," *PMLA*, 82 (1967), 117-20.

[9] In his analysis of EDA, ("Structure and Meaning . . ."), Dudley attempts a study of the structure and the role of each character. He sees the work, however, as a progression towards an ultimate fusion of images, in particular, the view of love as seen in court and country.

[10] Northrop Frye, *The Secular Scripture: A Study of the Structure of Romance* (Cambridge, MA: Harvard University Press, 1976; rpt. 1978). Any references to the structure of romance or its literary conventions are based on this study.

ending (or a sad one), but goes on to link two narratives, resolve them both harmoniously and, in a convincing literary coup, provide the key to the resolution of the conflict in the frame story. The tale begins with the splintering of two families over their children's love affair and ends with the lovers' tomb becoming a shrine. As if this were not enough, the narrator tells us that the pilgrimages to the shrine gave rise to a village, which in turn produced a venerable, thriving port city. He recounts to us two variant versions of the story, proving beyond a doubt that the "history" has diffused into legend. When we recall the conventions of the structure of romance, there can be no doubt that this story, which is resolved harmoniously, is an affirmation, a celebration of its theme: love and loyalty.[11]

King Croes of Mondoya disapproves of the love that Ardanlier, his son, feels for Liessa, the daughter of "el grand señor de Lira" (p. 54). Fearing punishnment for their love, Ardanlier and Liessa flee, taking with them the faithful servant Lamidoras and the slave Bandyn. They travel to foreign courts and, in France, Ardanlier's prowess in jousts and tournaments is recognized, as is the beauty and gentility of Liessa. Princess Yrena falls in love with Ardanlier, who gently tells her that he must remain faithful to Liessa. Nevertheless, Yrena entrusts Ardanlier with the key to her heart—actually the key to a locket. Ardanlier and Liessa journey to Galicia, to a bucolic paradise where they build a subterranean palace. Their secret existence is safe for seven years until King Croes, who has been searching to avenge his son's disappearance, recognizes Ardanlier's dogs, and finds and kills the pregnant Liessa while Ardanlier is absent from the palace. Upon returning, Ardanlier, thinking that Lamidoras is responsible, in some way, for Liessa's death, berates him for his lack of loyalty. Upon hearing the true story of the murder, he writes to Yrena to free her from her self-imposed bondage, and kills himself, denouncing his father to the end. The story could have ended here, especially if it were meant to be a negative *exemplum*, but it does not.[12]

Lamidoras, the faithful servant, brings the news to Yrena and the court. Thrown into turmoil by the news, the court goes into mourning (paralleling the scene of nature gone wild at the secret palace). Yrena vows to redeem the lovers, pledges herself to chastity, sends Lamidoras

---

[11] The theme of loyalty is convincingly discussed by Impey in "Ovid, Alfonso X...," pp. 291-94.
[12] See Andrachuk, "The Function of EDA...," p. 29.

to the Holy Roman Emperor, who denounces King Croes, and journeys, accompanied by maidens garbed in black, to the palace-cum-tomb
of the lovers, where she is later joined by Lamidoras. By enchantment
Yrena seals the tomb, to be opened only by the most loyal lover the
world has known. Lamidoras dies and is interred in the first room;
Yrena, upon her death, in the second; the lovers lie beyond, in the third
room. Knights of all degree attempt to penetrate the tomb but not
until Macías arrives, the most loyal, noble, heroic lover of them all (at
least, to our author), is the spell broken. The tomb is disenchanted,
opening three times each year for pilgrims—on May 1, June 24, and
July 25. Later, the site is so popular that a village springs up, which
grows to be a coastal metropolis. The story ends with a variation of the
legend surrounding the hunting dogs of Ardanlier, and the narrator's
assertion that he is himself a direct descendant of Macías, inheriting
from him the virtue of loyalty.

EDA roughly divides itself into eighteen sections which alternate
stasis and motion (journeys):

1. Ardanlier and Liessa fall in love in Mondoya; parents disapprove
2. Flight to foreign courts
3. Time in the courts; Yrena falls in love
4. Journey to retreat (secret palace)
5. Building of and time within the palace
6. Journey of father; Ardanlier goes hunting
7. Murder of Liessa
8. Father departs; Ardanlier returns
9. Death of Ardanlier
10. Lamidoras goes to the court
11. Court description
12. Lamidoras goes to the Emperor (Yrena goes to secret palace)
13. Court description
14. Lamidoras goes to the secret palace (Yrena constructs tomb)
15. Interment of Lamidoras and Yrena in palace/tomb
16. Mention of great number of foreign visitors and their un-
    successful attempts to penetrate tomb
17. Salvation by Macías (penetration of tomb)
18. Descriptions of pilgrimages to the tomb, followed by the growth
    of the city around it, and, finally, the development and diffu-
    sion of the legend.

The balance achieved by this structure is striking. The journey of

Lamidoras to the court is almost the exact center of the work: *EDA* is almost perfectly divided into two narratives. Other interesting features are the combination of journeys in one time period, and the contrast of the description of one person's journey with reference to another's static event. For example, Yrena sends Lamidoras to the Emperor while she goes to the secret palace, and, in number 8, the father is departing at the same time Ardanlier is making his way back to the palace. Episodes 6-14 form an interesting balance. Scenes 6 and 8 are offset by the murder of Liessa by the father. Both scenes illustrate two actions of the same people, the king and Ardanlier. The death of Ardanlier occurs, then the central action of Lamidoras' linking of the two narratives. In the new narrative, a similar balance is seen: the court description (the news of Ardanlier's suicide and Liessa's murder) follows the central episode, scene 10, then continues with a balance of three episodes. Scenes 12 and 14, both involving Yrena and Lamidoras, surround the description of Lamidoras' arrival at the court of the Emperor and the Emperor's raging epistolary denunciation of King Croes' vile actions. Scenes 7 and 13 are offset by parallel journeys, and both deal with the murder of Liessa and deal directly with King Croes. This tends to create a highly concentrated sense of drama in the center of the work.

Scenes 16 and 17 maintain the contrast of stasis and motion in a different way from the other scenes. In order to highlight Macías' success in contrast to the high number of failed attempts, the narrator makes the point that they came from far away but spares few words to describe how far they were able to get in the enchanted tomb:

> Ninguno passava ni podia tocar al primero y segundo por mas que llegava; e grandes prinçipes affricanos, de Asya y Europa, reyes, duques, condes, caualleros, marqueses y gentiles omnes, lyndas damas de leuante y poniente, meridion y sententryon, con saluo conduto del grand Rey despaña venian en prueva de aquesta aventura... Sola tristeza, peligro y afan, por mas que pugnavan, avian por gloria; ... (pp. 71-72)

The arrival of Macías, on the other hand, is described only in passing in order to get to the point. The above quotation continues:

> fasta grand cuento de años quel buen Maçias, gadisan del aguila, naçido enlas faldas dessa agra montaña, por su grand gentileza, lealtat, destreza y grand fortaleza, viniendo en conquista del primer aloje, dyo franco paso al segundo albergue. (p. 72)

Macías enters effortlessly where the others could not, and the tomb ceases to be enchanted. Thus, the final description is one of great joy because of the growth of the city and the legend.

The actions of Ardanlier and Liessa and Yrena can be described in terms of high points and low points:

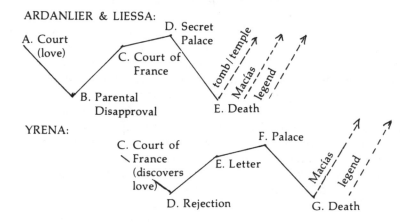

Lamidoras' actions link the two points labeled E, causing him to begin his function as the narrator of the tale and as the link between the two sections. He alone can inform the bewildered and despairing Ardanlier of the murder and, when Ardanlier perishes, carry the tale to Yrena and the court. It is Lamidoras' role as the perfect messenger, the loyal servant, that keeps the narrative from ending simply as romance conventions inverted. The lovers will be avenged, not by the death of King Croes, although by the Emperor's decree he becomes the enemy of the work, but through the efforts of Yrena to enshrine the bodies of the lovers and ensure their eternal peace and adulation. The lowest point for Ardanlier and Liessa, their deaths, signals an upswing for Yrena, who will be able to prove her fidelity. Although they are unaware of it, the deaths of Ardanlier and Liessa are an upswing also, since they set in motion the events which will result in their glorification. Yrena's next action (F), is on a higher plane than is E: actions speak louder than words and she has complied with the promise to redeem the lovers. The low point (G) follows, but the sorrow rapidly turns to celebration when Macías undertakes the challenge. There is

complete resolution: Macías succeeds and raises all those buried within
to a sacred level, now worshiped by all the world's lovers. This
vindicates, as much as possible, the deaths of Ardanlier and Liessa, and
validates the chaste love that Yrena embodied. Court and country
intermingle by the sharing of the tomb which is now the object of a
pilgrimage.

Among the other balancing techniques employed by Rodríguez del
Padrón are parallel journeys and descriptions (such as the ones mentioned above), the fusion of the secular and the sacred, and the use of
dialogue.[13]

Nature goes wild in response to the deaths of Ardanlier and Liessa.
This change in nature has a parallel in the courtly response.[14] It is
more, however, than simply a change of clothing from first of May
celebrations to mourning attire: the court goes wild as does nature.
Nature was so disturbed that "el mundo penso feneçer" (p. 65). The
court, seeing "el no desconoçido ayo del famoso Ardanlier, tan desse-
ado, esperado aquel dia, maravillados, çercandolo de todas partes" (p.
65) mirrors the actions of the forest creatures incredulously approaching the dead bodies from all sides: "las lyndas aves de rrapinia
quebrantan las lonjas con las pyhuelas, solas dexan las alcandaras, e
çercan de todas partes los dos cuerpos inanimables" (p. 64). Devastated
by the news, Yrena faints and, when she is revived, vows to dedicate
the palace to "la muy clara Vesta, deessa de castidat, con promessa de
visitar el nombrado sepulchro del su buen amigo Ardanlyer, y hazer del
soterraño palaçio templo solenne a honor de aquella" (p. 66), since she,
like Ardanlier, cannot abandon the love she has felt, but must remain
loyal, even if only to a memory. Accompanied by devout virgins, she
plans to go on a pilgrimage but first arranges with Lamidoras that he

---

[13] In "Structure and Meaning" (pp. 113-25), Dudley divides the entirety of
*EDA* by "Author speaks, character speaks" even when it is narration. He tells
us that there are only eight direct utterances in the text, alternating with
narration, all concerned with the death of Liessa (pp. 121-22). The alternating
use of dialogue and narration for numbers 7-13 of my own division is useful,
and demonstrates Juan Rodríguez' effective use of dialogue. I find it pointless,
however, to refer to the whole narration from the beginning of the text to
the king's speech and from Lamidoras' sea-journey to the palace/tomb to the
end of the text simply as "Author speaks."

[14] Dudley, "Court and Country," p. 119: "A change in the appearance of
nature begins immediately after the deaths of Ardanlier and Liessa. The same
kind of change is found in the courtly pattern but without any hint of
supernatural phenomenon."

bear the news to the Emperor and give Bandyn to her in order to lead them to the secret palace. The Emperor declares himself to be completely against King Croes, calling him his greatest enemy, thereby making him the enemy of many courts: the courtly equivalent of the disturbance of nature. The natural world and the ordered one are in agreement in their reverence for Ardanlier and Liessa's love.

Because of this union of belief, it seems a somewhat simplistic, or overly rigorous, notion to view the court as representative of frustrated love, as Dudley (p. 119) sees it, and nature as the place of fulfilled love. Yrena does represent the kind of courtly experience that is seen in *cancionero* and troubadour poetry, and in the author's frame story, but there is little indication that the courts, except for Mondoya, are hostile to the kind of love existing between Ardanlier and Liessa. On the contrary, the similarity of reaction between the courtly world and the natural world demonstrates an affinity of understanding. The court is sorrowful, not due to the respect it has for Yrena's courtly worship of Ardanlier, but because it recognizes the value of the two lovers and of their love. In fact, in the epistle from the Emperor to King Croes, his "capital enemigo," the Emperor mentions the death of Ardanlier but gives more time to a lament for Liessa's death. Then:

> por todo el Ymperio, sus reynos, ducados, condados, prinçipados y tierras, mando aclarar su contrario, capital enemigo del rey Croes de Mondoya, haziendo juras, votos, promessas, de vengar la tan syn piedat muerte que el lleno de toda crueldat asy diera ala ynoçente Lyessa. (p. 68)

Most roads in *EDA* seem to lead to the secret palace. Ardanlier and Liessa's journey and search for a retreat is paralleled in intent by Yrena's: they seek to create, uplift, to restore harmony. The father's journey of destruction is offset by that of Macías' journey to the tomb, and both journeys are described as penetrations. The description of Liessa's murder, because it is a dramatic high point of the text, receives much more attention:

> El muy lastymado Rey no pudo durar que no fuese enla busca; e despues delos grandes affanes que no se suelen asconder alos viandantes, pasados luengos dias, meses, cuento de años, que andaua en su demanda, quiso ventura que vyniendo de passo dela antiga çibdat de Venera, quanto vna legua del secreto palaçio, vio venir los tres canes ladrando por la angosta senda, las gargantas abiertas, llenas de sangre, encarnados de vn fiero dayne que su hijo Ardanlier essas horas muerto avia, que solo quedaua enel monte adereçando

por lo traer detras de sy enla rropa del brioso cauallo que dubdaua de lo consentyr. Al trabajado Rey bien plogo delos seguir, dubdando la casta delos perros que conoçer queria; e fueron por la estrecha via ferir ala secreta casa que no avian por saber...Dando fyn alas dolorosas palabras, el ynfamado de grand crueldat tendio la aguda espada, y siguio vna falssa punta que le atraueso las entrañas, atrauesando por medio dela criatura; e tendida enel suelo, dio el trabajado espiritu. (pp. 57-58)

The father searches for many years for his son and Liessa. As he nears the end of his search, and comes closer and closer to finding them, the narration shows the closing-in by terms of geographical description— the King travels everywhere, then finds Venera, the city, then the forest, the dogs, the path, and, finally, the woman. The description ends with the narrowing of geographical space until it is a sword in Liessa's womb, dividing her child in half.

The disenchantment of the tomb by Macías is shorter, but the parallel of penetration is there:

Sola tristeza, peligro y afan, por mas que pugnavan, avian por gloria; fasta grand cuento de años quel buen Maçias, gadisan del aguila, naçido enlas faldas dessa agra montaña, por su grand gentileza, lealtat, destreza y grand fortaleza, viniendo en conquista del primer aloje, dyo franco paso al segundo albergue. Despues delos dos grandes peligros, contrastes, rreueses, pauores, affanes que el buen gadisan, gridando Bulcan, sufria por tocar al Padron, entrando el carçel, çesso el encanto, y la secreta camara fue conquistada. (p. 72)

Narrative space in general is very interesting in *EDA* since it moves from wide, universal spaces to a small space. However, the significance of that space changes, as in the transformational process from palace to tomb to shrine, the re-defining of what is primarily a secular space to a sacred one and, even stronger, to one of ritual.[15] When the palace is constructed it is, for all practical purposes, a secular space. It is a retreat for two lovers. Since, however, it is an edifice created within the vast expanse of a forest, there is a sacredness about it: "a sacred place constitutes a break in the homogeneity of space; this break is symbolized by an opening by which passage from one cosmic region to

15 Mircea Eliade, *The Sacred and the Profane: The Nature of Religion,* trans. Willard R. Trask (New York: Harcourt, Brace and World, 1959; rpt. Harcourt Brace Jovanovich, n.d.). See especially Chapter 1, "Sacred Space and Making the World Sacred," pp. 20-65.

another is made possible (from heaven to earth and vice versa; from earth to the underworld)," (Eliade, p. 37).

The subterranean palace is the setting, not for a mere passionate affair, but for the establishment of home, a fixed center in which a family resides: Liessa, when we next see her, is carrying Ardanlier's child. That King Croes ignores the life of the unborn child, dividing it in two as he stabs Liessa, could be seen as a contamination of the sacred place. However, it is interesting to note that the text very clearly states that King Croes comes upon Liessa outside the palace: Liessa and Lamidoras hear noises and, thinking that it is Ardanlier returning from the hunt, go outside to meet him. The threshold, by definition, marks the transition from one space to another, oftentimes from a secular to sacred space (Eliade, pp. 25-27). The idyllic retreat of Ardanlier and Liessa has indeed been violated but only up to a point: the sacred space, the templum of space, remains uncontaminated by the violence occurring just outside it.

Yrena decides to dedicate the newly-created sepulchre in the secret palace to the "deesa Vesta:" "E hecha la deuida salua, en rrecuentas delas aventuras, desçendieron [Yrena and her maidens] al nuevo templo de la deesa Vesta, do reynava la Deesa de amores" (p. 69). The text indicates that the palace already had been a sacred place of sorts, since the goddess of love had reigned there. This new transformation, from palace to temple, is a step towards affirming its sacredness.

When Macías breaks the enchantment, the palace/tomb becomes a ritual space. The boundary of the significance of the palace, as the lovers' home, and that of the tomb as merely a final resting place for four loyal people, is broken, taking on an enlarged, universal significance: that of the shrine. Ritual is attached to the edifice: the palace magically opens to pilgrims three times each year to commemorate its founding by Yrena, its disenchantment by Macías, and the love of Ardanlier and Liessa. The three dates, May 1, June 24 and July 25, tie *Estoria de dos amadores* to a mythic context. May 1 and June 24 are both important in amatory folklore. Springtime and fertility rituals are associated with May celebrations and in *EDA*, it is the day that Lamidoras brings to the court the news of the lovers' deaths. June 24, the feast of San Juan, is associated with the midsummer's night rituals of finding new love. As we will see, it may also merge in *EDA* with the legend of the Virgin of Liesse and therefore with Liessa. July 25, the feast of Santiago, the saint who inspired so many pilgrimages, further demonstrates Rodríguez del Padrón's attempts to fuse the sacred and the profane.[16]

If we are not already convinced of the universal importance of this edifice, the author makes it perfectly clear. The site of the pilgrimage draws such a multitude of people that a village grows up around it, eventually developing into a large city. Romance normally ends with a wedding, banquet, or some other show of social unity. Although EDA does not conform to this pattern in the usual way, there is, nonetheless, a community of solidarity: from two lovers fleeing the court of Mondoya, EDA moves consistently, in a peripatetic series of actions, towards a harmonious conclusion. The ritual space, which was once a palace, has gone outside of itself, or broken its boundaries by extending its significance, to spawn a city.

*Literary and Historical References: The Blending of Legends*

In the background of EDA, one finds a subtle blend of religious and secular analogues, which lend additional depth to the theme and structure. Some of the analogues are obvious: Dona Inês de Castro and Santiago are two Iberian figures mentioned by several critics.[17] Other analogues proposed are the Virgin Mary for Yrena and the name Liessa from the Virgin of Liesse.[18] María Rosa Lida de Malkiel, discussing the murder of Liessa, outlines the similarity of a section of *Baladro del sabio Merlín* to the narrative moments in EDA.[19] Marina Scordilis Brownlee develops the idea of a "Dantean subtext" and Olga Impey concluded

---

[16] Eliade discusses throughout *The Sacred and the Profane* the importance of ritual for the sanctity of edifices. The opening of the tomb three times a year is ritualistic, ensuring the return of the faithful to the building.

[17] This is almost a commonplace of *Siervo libre de amor* criticism, but for a description of the connection between the legend of Santiago and *Estoria de dos amadores*, see Gilderman, pp. 103-04 and for Inês de Castro elements, see Paz y Melia, p. xxi and Martin Nozick, "The Inez de Castro Theme in European Literature,' *CL*, 3 (1951), 330-41.

[18] Herrero, "The Allegorical Structure," pp. 761-62, sees Yrena as a nun dedicated to Mary—the triumph of Vesta over Diana as symbolic of the triumph of Mary over Venus. Paz y Melia suggests that the name Liessa has some connection with the legend of the Virgin of Liesse "aparecida en 1133 en el Cairo a unos caballeros de la orden de San Juan, los cuales dieron aquel nombre por el gozo que les causó" (p. 416).

[19] "Influencia," pp. 20-25. She says, "Es evidente que la combinación idéntica de idénticos motivos no puede ser un azar. Los dos relatos no son independientes. ¿Cuál de ellos ha sido el original? Dificulta el problema el no saber cómo era la versión del *Baladro* que circulaba en los tiempos de Juan Rodríguez del Padrón" (p. 21).

that the prose of Juan Rodríguez del Padrón has its origins in Ovid and Alfonso el Sabio and not, as claimed by many, in the Boccaccian *Fiammetta* and Aeneas Sylvius Piccolomini's *Historia de duobus amantibus*.[20] It is important to remember our author's interest in Latin and Italian authorities for he translated Ovid's *Heroides* into Spanish and invented three additional letters for the work. *EDA* exploits some well-known legends by comparing, contrasting, and modifying their content. It is interesting that no suggested analogue links, in any concrete way, the three protagonists: Ardanlier, Liessa, and Yrena. If we look to an earlier effort of Rodríguez del Padrón, *Carta de Madreselva a Mauseol*, one of the three letters added to the *Heroides*, we see the love triangle of Mauseol, Madreselva, and Artemisa. A possible analogue to that epistle and, ultimately, *EDA* is the Tristan legend.

The Tristan legend, judging by the texts and fragments of texts which have been discovered, was enormously popular, both as literature and as a social influence, giving rise to groups such as the Order of the Honeysuckle.[21] Madreselva, Spanish for honeysuckle, is most

---

[20] "Ovid, Alfonso X, ...". Also, in this regard, see Impey, "The Literary Emancipation...," in which she states: "They [earlier works of Juan Rodríguez] establish the continuity of Juan Rodríguez's literary activity and offer proof of the fact that the *Siervo libre* cannot be fully understood if it is severed from his other prose works; finally, they make abundantly clear the irrelevance of any detour through the prose of Boccaccio or Aeneas Sylvius Piccolomini as an explanation for certain aspects of the conception and composition of the *Siervo libre de amor*" (p. 315).

[21] We know that the Tristan legend was circulating at the time of Juan Rodríguez and even much earlier: "Although the twelfth-century Tristan poem of Thomas of Brittany certainly exerted influence outside French-speaking territory, particularly in Northern Europe, the international 'best seller' among the Tristan stories was without doubt the anonymous prose *Tristan*, with its emphasis on chivalric adventures and the Grail Quest. Translations and adaptations survive in full or in fragments in Serbo-Russian [presumably a printer's error for Serbo-Croatian, Russian], Danish, English, Italian, Catalan, Aragonese, Castilian, and Galician-Portuguese," Harvey L. Sharrer, "Malory and the Spanish and Italian Tristan Texts: The Search for the Missing Link," *Tristania*, 4, no. 2, (May 1979), 36-43, p. 37. For a detailed summary of the prose *Tristan*, see E. Löseth, *Le Roman en Prose de 'Tristan,' le roman de Palamède et la compilation de Rusticien de Pise, analyse critique d'après* les manuscrits de Paris, Bibliothèque de l'École des Hautes Études, 82 (Paris, 1891; rpt. New York: Burt Franklin, 1980). For a discussion of the problems associated with the examination of the sources and versions of the Tristan legend in Spain, see Pedro F. Campa, "The Spanish Tristán: Research and New Directions," *Tristania*, 3, no. 2, (May 1978), 36-45.

notably associated with *Chèvrefeuille* (French for honeysuckle), a *lai* of Marie de France about Tristan and Iseult. Charles V. Aubrun attributes Rodríguez del Padrón's choice of his protagonist's name— Madreselva—either to his knowledge of *Chèvrefeuille* or to his familiarity with the above-mentioned Order of the Honeysuckle.[22]

*Carta de Madreselva* is a missive against Mauseol and his actions, deemed by Madreselva to be a complete betrayal of their love. Madreselva, a queen, has been incarcerated by her mother, Adelfa, who discovered and disapproved of the love between her daughter and Mauseol. Madreselva learns that, in order to save himself, Mauseol has wedded another woman, Artemisa. Calling him a traitor, disloyal, unfeeling, Madreselva laments her fate and berates her lover in a moving epistle.

The Tristan legend offers a similar theme: Tristan loves Iseult of Cornwall completely, or so he says, yet, when he is offered in marriage Iseult of the White Hands, he marries, but soon learns that he must remain sexually loyal to his first love. Iseult of Cornwall, like Madreselva, rages on hearing the news that her lover has married. Again, like Madreselva, she directs an angry missive to the treacherous lover. Although, as is commonly known, this story continues and Iseult of the White Hands, unlike Yrena, betrays her beloved, its parallel with *Carta de Madreselva* ends here.

Rodríguez del Padrón, in what could be called a practice attempt for *EDA*, employed the very structure of the Tristan characters' relationship and a part of its theme in *Carta de Madreselva*. *EDA* represents an artistic and highly original renovation of the Tristan legend, especially its theme of loyalty.

In contrast, however, Ardanlier, the hero of *EDA*, is not the wavering Tristan. When faced with the temptation of a new love, one who loves him deeply, he remains loyal to his first love, Liessa—the one with whom he has a physical relationship. Ardanlier and Liessa flee to the country, as do Tristan and Queen Iseult, where both couples dwell in relative comfort. For Tristan and Iseult, since it is an adulterous affair and since, although this is less important, they live in

---

[22] In *Le Chansonnier espagnol d'Herberay des Essarts (XVᵉ siècle)* (Bordeaux: Féret, 1951), he has this to say: "Juan Rodríguez était Galicien. Sa culture, par ailleurs classique, embrassait également les romans bretons d'origine lyrique (lais de Marie de France) en faveur au Portugal. Il a pu encore se souvenir du premier ordre portugais des Chevaliers de la Madreselva, créé à la fin du XIVᵉ siècle, lors du mariage de Jean Iᵉʳ avec Catherine de Lancastre" (p. 206).

a dwelling-place created by "la sage demoiselle," there is a sense of hiding from society rather than creating their own in the manner of Ardanlier and Liessa. Both women are discovered when the men are out hunting, but the parallel stops there: Iseult is taken away from Le Morois, while Liessa and her unborn child are brutally slaughtered. Upon discovering Liessa's body, Ardanlier writes to his other love but vows that, through loyalty, which he owes to the goddess Minerva, he must follow his first love, even in death. Tristan, upon discovering Iseult's absence, laments, but is deterred during several adventures from finding her, one of the adventures being his marriage to Iseult of the White Hands.

Ardanlier and Liessa are buried in a sepulchre in their secret palace. Yrena, ever-faithful, sees to their burial.[23] She never knows the physical love of Ardanlier but, in spite of this, remains devoted to him. Iseult of the White Hands remained devoted to Tristan throughout their marriage, but betrays him with a lie at the end of his life. After the death of Tristan and Iseult, she sees to the burial of the lovers.[24]

In addition to the incorporation and modification of the Tristan legend, and perhaps Arthurian material in general, Rodríguez del Padrón merges other secular analogues with religious ones, and, in so

[23] In addition to the virtue of fidelity, Iseult of the White Hands and Yrena share a physical similarity. When Lamidoras brings Yrena the news of Ardanlier's death, there follows a description of Yrena which makes mention of her white hands: "Entrados ala postrymera camara, dando sus oydos ala triste embaxada, e la vista con el sentido ala amargosa epistola, mensagera de aquel, e hechura de sus propias manos, tendio muy sin piedat las muy lindas suyas, en grand estrago de sus cabellos, hilos de oro pareçientes, tyrando dellos muy sin dolor, firiendo enel real visaje, plegando las blancas manos, bolando el graçioso cuello, llorando, gymiendo, agramente sospirando, haziendo las vascas, fasta obmudecida caher enel rrico estrado syn sentido," p. 66.

[24] Unlike Yrena, who is unwaveringly devoted to Ardanlier in life and to Ardanlier and Liessa after their death, the case of Iseult of the White Hands is problematic. According to the prose *Tristan*, she is the indirect cause of Tristan's death since she lies to him about the color of the sail on the approaching ship. The sail was to be white if Queen Iseult were on the ship, black if she were not aboard. Iseult tells Tristan that the color is black, even though it is white, at which point Tristan despairs and expires. When Queen Iseult arrives and finds that Tristan has already died, she, too, expires. Tristan's wife orders the building of the tomb and the lovers' joint burial. It is uncertain whether she does this out of guilt over Tristan's death or out of devotion, as Yrena had done for Ardanlier and Liessa. For a summary of the death of Tristan and Iseult, see Löseth, section 54, pp. 44-45.

doing, attains for his protagonists such a level of purity and goodness that each one is deemed worthy of worship.

There is a tendency, justified by literary precedent, to view sensual love as sinful. It is often condemned by medieval authors (Dante's *Divina Commedia* is a good example); and women and sexual love are indissolubly linked to Eve and the downfall of man. In order to avoid this simple categorization of sex/sin/downfall, Rodríguez del Padrón endowed his somewhat one-dimensional character Liessa with the qualities of two extremely popular and sympathetic figures: the secular Inês de Castro and, more importantly, the Virgin Mary, and, in fact, appears to draw heavily from the theme and structure of the legend of the Virgin of Liesse.

In the court of France, Liessa is portrayed as a graceful, gentle and virtuous lover; she is later a mother pleading for her unborn child's life in the face of the cruelty of Ardanlier's father. Referring to the women of the court and their reverence for Liessa, the text states: "Magnificos señores, y todos los gentiles hombres lo [Ardanlier] aconpañauan y hazian estrañas caresas; e no menos por causa dela gentil Liessa, bien quista y guardada de todas las lindas damas, seruidoras dela Liessa, que de buena voluntat se dieran en troque por ella" (p. 55). This must be a reference to the cult of the Virgin of Liesse, suggested by the heroine's name, *liessa, alegría*.

The legend tells of three French knights, from the Order of St. John, who fall captive to the Sultan in Cairo. The Sultan's beautiful daughter, Ismeria, sent by her father to the prison in order to convert the knights to Islam, is instead converted to Christianity when the Knights recount the story of Mary, especially the Nativity, and her attempts to protect her child. The Virgin's image appears on a piece of wood and the four are miraculously delivered from the prison to the shore, where a boat, again, miraculously, appears out of nowhere and transports them to France. Here, in honor of the Virgin, they build a church and name it in honor of joy, *liesse*.[25] This legend enjoyed great popularity through the seventeenth century, and even served as a source for Cervantes' "Captive's Tale" in *Don Quijote*.[26]

The point is being driven home that we are to see Liessa as a figure

[25] For a summary of the legend and its popularity in Spain, see Georges Cirot, "Le 'Cautivo' de Cervantes et Notre-Dame de Liesse," *BH*, 38 (1936), 378-82.

[26] See Cirot, above, and Alban K. Forcione, *Cervantes and the Humanist Vision: A Study of Four "Exemplary Novels"* (Princeton: University Press, 1982), pp. 347-48.

of worship. It is a subtle means of elevating the esteem of Liessa in our eyes, the results of which are three: we see a love affair of equals, not of a king's son and an inferior woman; there are the beginnings of a fusion between the chivalric, represented by Ardanlier, and the sacred, represented by Liessa, a fusion which is a fundamental technique throughout the work; and, the violence strikes us as all the more shocking because the love does not seem to have offended a law of society. On the contrary, the courts of the world, with the obvious exception of Mondoya, are delighted by their love.

After Ardanlier and Liessa have lived in the subterranean palace for several years, a transformation takes place: Liessa becomes a Madonna figure, again, through her association with the story of Mary recounted to Ismeria. When her plea for clemency for herself and her unborn child goes unheeded by the vengeful parent, King Croes, and she and her child are murdered, the sense of horror is heightened by the author's having infused the character of Liessa with religious overtones.

It is not unusual to find a dichotomy between the good woman and the bad woman, as exemplified by Mary and Eve, or, as Frye calls the distinction, fair and dark heroines.[27] The bad woman, whose sensuality brings about man's downfall, is contrasted with the pure, good woman. Here, Yrena embodies the qualities of the good woman, the courtly lover who is sexually pure, who is normally the Marian figure. But Rodríguez del Padrón avoids the rigid association of bad woman and sexual activity by endowing both women, Liessa and Yrena, with qualities associated with Mary. There is no doubt that Yrena and Ardanlier's love for each other occupied a different plane from that of the same hero and Liessa—love from afar and love which includes a sexual relationship are quite obviously different—but Rodríguez del Padrón went to great lengths to avoid creating an unfathomable abyss between the two.

Explicit descriptions of passionate encounters find no place in *EDA*. Obviously, since Liessa was pregnant, some sexual activity had taken place. But, as Impey points out, the references to Ardanlier and Liessa's love rarely surpass such moderate statements as "aquella que amaua mas que a sy' (p. 56).[28] Also, the father disapproved, but the courts of Europe in general were not averse to this love, judging

[27] Frye, *The Secular Scripture*. A discussion of the significance of the heroine in romance can be found throughout the study, but especially in Chapters 2-4, pp. 65-157.

[28] "Ovid, Alfonso X...," p. 292.

by their acceptance of Ardanlier and Liessa and the Emperor's denunciation of King Croes.

When Paz y Melia mentioned in passing (p. 416) the Virgin of Liesse, he did not know how many textual associations there are with the legend. Yrena becomes a spiritual deliverer of Ardanlier and Liessa by setting out on a pilgrimage and establishing a shrine, a sanctuary, a kind of *Church* to Liessa. The three days on which the tomb magically opens—May 1, June 24, the feast of San Juan, (remember, too, that the French knights were of the Order of St. John), and July 25—are even more closely linked in medieval minds than we may have suspected. As Egla Morales Blouin tells us:

> Las fiestas de San Juan se entremezclan y se confunden constantemente con las de mayo, especialmente en cuanto ambas comparten una serie de actividades de origen mítico que corresponden al simbolismo solsticial de agua y fuego. El agua de mayo era casi tan milagrosa como la de San Juan, embelleciendo, fertilizando, y tan preciada, que se conservaba para usos curativos y prodigiosos.[29]

She goes on to say that San Juan and Santiago were often confused:

> La propensión a recalcar las relaciones míticas entre San Juan y Cristo recuerdan a los innumerables gemelos divinos de las diversas mitologías, y la discusión de Américo Castro respecto a la interpretación popular del apóstol Santiago como hermano o aún gemelo de Cristo. Esta cuestión es especialmente interesante en vista de que la lírica muestra cierta tendencia a confundir a San Juan con Santiago. (p. 257)

*Estoria de dos amadores* functions, then, on one level very much as a miracle narrative. Liessa, the heroine, inspires tremendous devotion, a *religion of love*, as evidenced by the fusion of sacred and profane elements throughout the text.

In conclusion, we can say that *EDA* is a complex, carefully-constructed narrative designed to bring about a harmonious resolution in spite of the deaths of the lovers. Unlike the lovers of *Fiammetta* or *Divina Commedia*, for example, Ardanlier and Liessa are not portrayed as culpable sinners who are carried away by desire. Certainly desire initiates the action, although we are told that fear sets in motion the story of their flight; "las fuerças del temor acreçentaua[n]

---

[29] *El ciervo y la fuente: mito y folklore del agua en la lírica tradicional,* Studia Humanitatis (Madrid: José Porrúa Turanzas, 1981), p. 275.

enlos coraçones de aquellos las grandes furias del amor" (p. 54). But there is no indication that their love is sinful. Yrena spiritually avenges the lovers' deaths and, in so doing, proves herself to be worthy to join them in the shrine.

This kind of vindication is not without literary precedent. In his article on the moral question of suicide in the writings of Christian authors, Daniel Rolfs has this to say about Boccaccio:

> Boccaccio's frequent use of the theme of suicide throughout the *Decameron* emphasizes and pays tribute to this very concept of love as an undeniable force which operates independently of man's reason, social institutions and morality, a force which cares nothing for whatever obstacles foolish men and women place in its path. Its triumph is of course a happy one when those who oppose its will can be made to yield, but Love will have its way even when such is not possible, though in this latter instance its will can be served only by means of the supreme protest of suicide. Those who choose this protest serve a harsh master, but a just one, since in exchange for their affirmation of love and their loyalty to their own nature, they are rewarded in death if not life. In two of the tales to be discussed which end in double tragedy, the ill-fated lovers are buried together by a grieved community so that the union they vainly sought in life is finally made eternal. But even when this is not the case, their love is often vindicated and honored by all, even those who once most opposed it. Justice is further served by the protest of suicide with regard to this latter group, in that the opponents of Love are either punished with the loss of someone dear to them, or are at least exposed for their ignorance and cruelty.[30]

Rolf's example from *Decameron* fits very well with the events of *Estoria de dos amadores*, in which the lovers are indeed vindicated, honored and celebrated. Had the story stopped with the suicide of Ardanlier, then perhaps *EDA* could have been seen as a negative *exemplum*, but everything in the story points to a harmonious resolution. Beyond a shadow of a doubt, the overriding theme of *EDA* is loyalty and redemption, that of the love servant, the loyal lovers, and even the faithful vassal, Lamidoras.

[30] "Dante, Petrarch, Boccaccio and the Problem of Suicide," *RR*, 67 (1976), 200-25, p. 218.

*The Resolution of "Estoria de dos amadores" and the Frame Story*

Although Ardanlier and Liessa die, their story is a successful *exemplum* of loyalty which resolves, or provides a key to, the frame story which surrounds it:

> The male protagonist is profoundly loyal: as we learn, in the *Siervo libre*, Siervo is guilty of indiscretion not of disloyalty; his aim throughout the romance is to prove this, not by a direct declaration but by the narration of another love story. Significantly, the conclusion of this story calls attention to the fact that his kinship with Macías and other great lovers is due to his loyalty: "he sólo heredado en su lealtad" (*SLA*, 106). Siervo's message is clear: his own "nombradía" (*SLA*, 106) or fame lies not in a great love that would end in selfsacrifice or destruction, but in the faithfulness he has shown throughout his life. At the end of the first part of the work, where his love with the unknown lady is treated, we learn that he has retired to the "templo de la grand soledat" not only for shame of having betrayed her name, but also out of *lealtat* (*SLA*, 75). In brief, the main theme—with only a few variations—of the *Siervo libre* is loyalty: that of the protagonist for the unknown lady; that of his enviable alter-ego, Ardanlier, for his spouse-like beloved, Liessa; that of Yrena for Ardanlier; that of Lamidoras for his master; even that of the thirteen hounds...which, stricken with grief at Ardanlier's death, turn to stone in front of his tomb (*SLA*, 106).[31]

Ardanlier invokes Minerva (wisdom) before he kills himself; Siervo awakes from his dream-sleep to follow the path of the "verde olyva, consagrada a Minerua" (p. 75). He then encounters Synderesis—wisdom personified—whose appearance as a redeemer of sorts relates her to both Liesse (as in the Virgin of Liesse, spiritual deliverer of captives) and Yrena (spiritual redeemer).

Disloyalty is embodied by the character of King Croes, referred to as "el segundo Nero" (p. 61), and the friend who betrays Siervo's confidence, about whom it is said: "E veyendo, syn mas lo dezir, que ninguno remediar me podia, al piadoso maestro de Nero, inuentor delas crueldades, eligiendo vn amigo discreto" (p. 44).

Structurally, there are certain similarities between the frame story and *EDA*: the love Siervo and his lady share is destroyed by the disloyal messenger; Ardanlier and Liessa know the joy and confidence of having a loyal love-servant and messenger—Lamidoras.

---

[31] Impey, "Ovid, Alfonso X...," p. 293.

Ardanlier and Siervo both have spiritual redeemers—Yrena and Synderesis. When Siervo awakes and realizes that all is not lost if he recalls and retains his heritage from Macías—loyalty—Synderesis, like Yrena for Ardanlier, is present to aid him. She arrives with her maidens by a sea voyage, as does Yrena. The black clothes, the allegorical name, the sudden appearance on the sea, all constitute an atmosphere of mystery which is far removed from the commonplace. It suggests a similarity between Yrena and the role of enchantment in the second part of *EDA* and the arrival of Synderesis for the latter half of the frame story.

*Siervo libre de amor* is a text of fusion and linkage--Lamidoras, as messenger, links the two narratives of *Estoria de dos amadores; Estoria de dos amadores* is linked to the frame story. The frame story is cyclical since we realize that, when Synderesis asks Siervo to recount his adventures, he will, no doubt, tell her what we, the readers, have just read.[32] There is a sense of the continuation of the work, not in more adventures, but in the countless retelling of the tale. It is told to Synderesis, we assume, to Gonzalo de Medina, and, finally, to his readers. Similarly, *EDA* results in the diffusion of legend and the growth of a port city—in terms of continuation, the story, legend, will spread and the city will grow commercially and in population. The notion of boundary is essential to the understanding of *EDA*, as shown above, and, ultimately, *Siervo libre de amor* as a whole: both sections, *EDA* and the frame story, create, extend and break boundaries in order to elevate the narrative to legend and link the intercalated story to the frame story.

When he awakes from his dream-sleep, Siervo cries out:

Buelta, buelta mi esquyvo pensar, dela deçiente via de perdiçion quel arbol populo, consagrado a Hercules, le demostrava al seguir de los tres caminos en el jardyn dela ventura; e prende la muy agra senda donde era la verde olyva, consagrada a Minerua, quel entendimiento nos enseñava quando partyo airado de mi. (p. 75)

He continues by reciting two poems, the first of which follows the theme of his love-captivity: "Avnque me vedes asy/catyvo, libre naçy" (p. 75). The second poem contains the following advice and Siervo's response to it:

[32] "Thus, the circle closes; the Author recovers his Understanding as he looks back over the story of his love and attempts to find the meaning of his own experience. The third stage of love is the act of literary creation" (Dudley, "Structure and Meaning," p. 162).

> Por una rybera verde,
> oy loar con mesura
> vn gayo dentre las flores,
> calandrias y ruyseñores
> por essa mesma fygura.
>
> E en son de alabança
> dezia vn discor:
> Servid al Señor,
> pobres de andança.
> Y yo por locura
> cante por amores,
> pobre de fauores,
> mas no de tristura. (p. 78)

There are three points to consider in drawing any conclusions about the intention of the work. First, the lesson that Siervo learns from *EDA* is that his inheritance from Macías is the virtue of loyalty. Second, he awakes "como de un graue sueño" (p. 75). Although he is still a captive of love, he recalls, in the above-mentioned poem, that he was not always one. Moreover, this poem is followed by the one containing the advice: "Servid al Señor." Third, immediately following the second poem, there is another description of going from darkness to light in both a literal and metaphorical sense:

> E assy errado por las malezas, mudado enlas mas altas arbores de mi escura maginança, por devisar algun poblado, falleme ribera del grand mar, en vista de vna grand vrca de armada. (p. 79)

At this point, Siervo finds himself on the shore, where he watches the arrival by sea of the mysterious Synderesis, to whom he will recount his adventures.

Even if Siervo should decide not to continue in love service, which is strongly suggested by the idea of awakening from a dream-sleep, and moving from overgrown land to the shore, and to devote himself to the service of God, we do not have to see in *Siervo libre de amor* a didactic intention to repudiate most of its content—courtly or worldly love. *Siervo libre de amor* is a personal account of the psychological reconciliation of the circumstances of an unhappy love affair. Because of the significance of *EDA*—the triumph of loyalty and Siervo's subsequent recognition of his own quality of loyalty—he can absolve himself of guilt and go on with his life.

*Estoria de dos amadores*, instead of being a negative *exemplum*, is rather a counter-*exemplum*. It is a tale of tragedy realized, yet vindicated, and the frame story can be seen as tragedy averted.[33] Siervo may find a higher plane for his need to love, in his pursuit of God, but this realization of what we might call a hierarchy of love service does not, of necessity, require a condemnation of other kinds of love service.

While one kind of love may be rejected in favor of a higher love, they are not morally antithetical. Marina Scordilis Brownlee's study is important because it convincingly explores the allegorical features of the first part of the work and *EDA*, and explains their significance in the context of a reworking of Dante's *Commedia*. Brownlee rightly sees the last part of *Siervo libre* as a celebration of the poet-narrator's recovered reason and as part of a spiritual progression to a higher love. This makes sense, but we must see it in terms of earthly love (good) and love of God (better), rather than the outright condemnation of earthly love. To see *EDA* as something to be totally rejected fails to take into account the growth and positive nature of what occurs after the lovers' deaths.

---

[33] Rolfs gives an example (p. 220) of the story within a story from the *Decameron* (V.8) in which the inner tale provides the moral and the outer shows the lesson put into practice. Each tale concerns the idea of self-destruction and the point is that the protagonist of the outer tale learns from the inner tale. This is notably similar to the structure of *Siervo libre de amor*.

# 2

# Desire and the Jealous Rival in Diego de San Pedro's Romances

IEGO DE SAN PEDRO IS most readily associated with his sentimental romance *Cárcel de Amor*.[1] His earlier romance, *Tractado de amores de Arnalte y Lucenda*, was first printed in 1491 for Queen Isabella and the ladies of her court. Not as popular as *Cárcel de Amor*, *Arnalte y Lucenda* went through four Spanish editions as compared to *Cárcel de Amor*'s twenty-four. However, half a century later, in 1543, *Arnalte y Lucenda* became the first Spanish work of fiction to be printed in England.[2]

Modern critics share fifteenth and sixteenth-century Spain's preference for *Cárcel de Amor*. They have tended to focus on *Arnalte y Lucenda* as the initial impulse of *Cárcel de Amor* without the latter's laudable stylistic and rhetorical achievements. Menéndez y Pelayo, who had read *Arnalte y Lucenda* only in its French and Italian translations, had this

---

[1] For a discussion of the problems involved in sorting out the various fifteenth-century San Pedros, see Keith Whinnom's excellent introduction to San Pedro's *Obras completas*, I: *Tractado de amores de Arnalte y Lucenda y Sermón*, Clásicos Castalia, 54 (Madrid: Castalia, 1973), pp. 9-34. All quotations from *Arnalte y Lucenda* are from this edition. Quotations from *Cárcel de Amor* will be from Whinnom's edition of the second volume of San Pedro's complete works, Clásicos Castalia, 39 (Madrid: Castalia, 1971). I do not reproduce Whinnom's brackets around his emendations.

[2] Dale B. J. Randall, *The Golden Tapestry: A Critical Survey of Non-Chivalric Spanish Fiction in English Translation (1543-1657)* (Durham, N. C.: Duke University Press, 1963), p. 39.

to say: "La fábula de esta novelita, que Diego de San Pedro fingió haber traducido del griego, es muy semejante a la de *Cárcel de Amor*, y puede considerarse como su primer esbozo."[3] While many critics have analyzed *Cárcel de Amor*, the analyses of *Arnalte y Lucenda* mostly consist of a listing of structural and plot similarities with *Cárcel de Amor* and a general dismissal of the value of *Arnalte y Lucenda* except as a dry run for *Cárcel de Amor*.[4] Four critics, in dealing with San Pedro's works, treat *Arnalte y Lucenda* more specifically than do others, although all four-- Keith Whinnom, Carmelo Samonà, Regula Langbehn-Rohland, and Pamela Waley—still agree on the superiority of *Cárcel de Amor*. As Whinnom says: "No quiero insistir en los defectos de *Arnalte y Lucenda*, que tiene méritos nada despreciables, sobre todo en el estilo y contenido de los discursos apasionados de Arnalte: pero conviene poner de relieve la gran superioridad de la *Cárcel de Amor*."[5]

---

[3] *Orígenes de la novela*, II (1907, rpt. Madrid: CSIC, 1943), pp. 33-34. That he had not read *Arnalte y Lucenda* in Spanish is obvious since he believes that San Pedro claimed to translate a Greek work. This is not the case in the Spanish version, but was added by the French and English translators, no doubt because the story takes place in Thebes and its environs. In fact, by 1660, in another English version of *Arnalte y Lucenda*, Randall tells us (p. 67), San Pedro was considered to be one of several translators in a series and is referred to only as "some Spaniard."

[4] Armando Durán, whose categories of sentimental romance obscure the issue rather than elucidate it, reduces the structure of both *Arnalte y Lucenda* and *Cárcel de Amor* to five main events (Arnalte, enamorado de Lucenda, es rechazado por la joven; Leriano, enamorado de Laureola, es rechazado por la joven, etc.) in *Estructura y técnicas de la novela sentimental y caballeresca* (Madrid: Gredos, 1973), pp. 24-29. Dorothy Sherman Severin goes much further, in "Structure and Thematic Repetitions in Diego de San Pedro's *Cárcel de Amor* and *Arnalte y Lucenda*," *HR*, 45 (1977), 165-69, by providing us with a detailed list of the opening events of the work, the letters and meetings between the characters, and the closing events. Severin's chart is useful since, for one, it shows the similarity of the structure of the opening and closing, but in general it gives a false impression of the work as a whole. Severin gives no account of the strict narration which occurs when Arnalte is describing what led to each letter and meeting. At times these narrations relate events in themselves, such as the joust and mumming. Therefore, the chart should be modified to indicate the quantity of narration, important in itself as a structural device.

[5] *Arnalte y Lucenda*, p. 63. For a study of stylistic differences between *Arnalte y Lucenda* and *Cárcel de Amor*, see Carmelo Samonà, "Diego de San Pedro: dall'*Arnalte y Lucenda* alla *Cárcel de Amor*," in *Studi in onore di Pietro Silva* (Florence: Felice le Monnier, 1957), pp. 261-77. Regula Langbehn-Rohland has produced a careful study of San Pedro's works, *Zur Interpretation der Romane des Diego de San Pedro*

Of the sentimental romances considered in this study, *Cárcel de Amor* is by far the favorite of the critics in terms of the quantity of books and articles it has provoked.[6] The interest in *Cárcel* is not surprising, since the text is rich not only in its employ of rhetorical devices, but in its allusions to other works, and most specifically, the role of the narrator as character.[7] For Hispanists specializing in areas other than medieval literature, and, especially, the casual reader of each century's high-lights, this interest is misleading given that *Cárcel de Amor* and, to a lesser extent, *Arnalte y Lucenda*, are quite unlike the other romances in the Spanish sentimental genre. In fact, one of the pitfalls of criticism of the genre is to see *Cárcel de Amor* as the standard of the group, thereby implying that other sentimental romances are measured by their proximity to the form and content of Diego de San Pedro's two works. Moreover, it becomes quite clear that the *modus operandi* of *Arnalte y Lucenda* and *Cárcel de Amor* is different from that of other sentimental romances.

Before examining the two texts, it is necessary to establish a critical framework which will be important not only for this chapter but for the study of *Grisel y Mirabella* and *Grimalte y Gradissa*. As we will see, the protagonists in San Pedro's writings suffer through the destructive

---

(Heidelberg: Carl Winter, 1970). See also Pamela Waley, "Love and Honour in the *Novelas sentimentales* of Juan de Flores and Diego de San Pedro," *BHS*, 43 (1966), pp. 253-75. See also Alfonso Rey "La primera persona narrativa en Diego de San Pedro," *BHS*, 58 (1981), 95-103.

[6] For bibliography on translations, editions and critical studies of *Cárcel de Amor*, see Whinnom's edition cited above. He has included in the third volume, in collaboration with Dorothy S. Severin, (*Poesías*, Clásicos Castalia, 98, 1979) corrections to his edition and additional bibliography. See also his *The Spanish Sentimental Romance 1440-1550: A Critical Bibliography*, Research Bibliographies and Checklists, 41 (London: Grant and Cutler, 1983).

[7] See, for example, Whinnom, Introduction to *Cárcel*, pp. 44-46, Joseph F. Chorpenning, "Rhetoric and Feminism in the *Cárcel de Amor*," *BHS*, 54 (1977), 1-8, and E. Michael Gerli, "Leriano's Libation: Notes on the *Cancionero* Lyric, *Ars Moriendi*, and the Probable Debt to Boccaccio," *MLN*, 96 (1981), 414-20. For a discussion of the role of the narrator in *Cárcel*, see Barbara F. Weissberger, "The Role of the *Auctor* in the Spanish Sentimental Novel," unpub. dissertation, Harvard University, 1976; Peter Dunn, "Narrator as Character in the *Cárcel de Amor*," *MLN*, 94 (1979), 187-99; Esther Tórrego, "Convención retórica y ficción narrativa en la *Cárcel de amor*," *NRFH*, 33 (1983), 330-39 and James Mandrell, "Author and Authority in *Cárcel de Amor*: The Role of El Auctor," *JHP*, 8 (1983-84), 99-122.

process of mimetic desire, described below, when the mimesis is the action of a real-life rival.

René Girard's studies of desire, most notably *Deceit, Desire and the Novel, Violence and the Sacred*, and *"To Double Business Bound"* are indispensable for the development of this chapter.[8] Girard reduces the workings of the heart to a socio-anthropological phenomenon. He claims that love spawns jealousy and rivalry and that people in love are either hoping to transform their being through love or merely following a role model of what they think is expected in love. Of major importance is his concept of triangular desire, that the desire of an object will arouse desire in a rival for that object.[9] The mediator, the third point of a love triangle, can be either a role model or an obstacle, usually a rival or cruel parent. Amadís was, for Don Quijote, a role model, but Elierso in *Arnalte* is an obstacle. Girard explains:

> The genius of Dante, like that of Cervantes, is bound up with the abandonment of the preconceptions of individualism. That is why the very essence of their genius has been misunderstood by the Romantics and their successors of today.
>
> Cervantes and Dante discover within the world of literature a whole territory of awareness that includes Shakespeare's "play within a play" and Gide's *mise en abîme*. The hero in the grip of some second-hand desire [one inspired by a book or a social system, such as courtly love] seeks to conquer the being, the essence of his model by as faithful an imitation as possible. If the hero lived in the same world as the model instead of being forever distanced from him by myth or history, as in the examples above [Don Quijote and Amadís, Paolo and Francesca reading Lancelot's story] he would necessarily come to desire the same object. The nearer the mediator, the more does the veneration that he inspires give way to hate and rivalry. Passion is no longer eternal.[10]

---

[8] *Violence and the Sacred*, trans. Patrick Gregory (Baltimore: Johns Hopkins University Press, 1977, rpt. 1979); *Deceit, Desire and the Novel: Self and Other in Literary Structure*, trans. Yvonne Freccero (Baltimore: Johns Hopkins University Press, 1966; rpt. 1980); *"To Double Business Bound": Essays on Literature, Mimesis, and Anthropology* (Baltimore: Johns Hopkins University Press, 1978). In addition, see his article "Myth and Ritual in Shakespeare: *A Midsummer Night's Dream*," in *Textual Strategies: Perspectives in Post Structuralist Criticism*, ed. Josué V. Harari (Ithaca: Cornell University Press, 1979; rpt. 1984), pp. 189-212.

[9] See especially "Triangular Desire," pp. 1-52, and "Men Become Gods in the Eyes of Each Other," pp. 53-82, both in *Deceit, Desire, and the Novel*.

[10] "The Mimetic Desire of Paolo and Francesca," in *"To Double Business Bound,"* p. 3.

Jealousy is part of the power of desire. Girard says that human beings traditionally explain away or defend jealousy of a rival by riveting attention on the qualities of the desired object:

> Jealousy and envy imply a third presence: object, subject, and a third person toward whom the jealousy or envy is directed. These two "vices" are therefore triangular; however we never recognize a model in the person who arouses jealousy because we always take a jealous person's attitude toward the problem of jealousy. Like all victims of internal mediation, the jealous person easily convinces himself that his desire is spontaneous, in other words, that it is deeply rooted in the object and the object alone. As a result he always maintains that his desire preceded the intervention of the mediator.[11]

Indeed, mimetic desire in one way or another is the byword in every one of the texts under consideration—in *Grisel y Mirabella*, for example, the introduction of Grisel to the story occurs when he kills his friend, a rival for Mirabella's love—but it does not alone constitute the action of the other tales. In San Pedro's works, however, the two male lovers, Arnalte and Leriano, are both thwarted by the intervention of a rival who causes the couple to break up: Elierso marries Arnalte's love, Lucenda, and a jealous Persio causes Leriano and Laureola to be accused of sexual transgressions.

In both *Cárcel de Amor* and *Arnalte y Lucenda* we will see triangular relationships which evolve from the harmless ones in which the lover follows a role model or employs a mediator, to those in which the lover encounters a rival or obstacle.

*The Evolution of "soledad," the Presence of the Jealous Rival, and Mimetic Desire in "Arnalte y Lucenda"*

For Pamela Waley, love and honor are the main theme of *Arnalte y Lucenda*, the counterpart of which is the poetry of the fifteenth-century *cancioneros*:

> It is obvious that the inspiration, the ideas, the motives and the expressions of Diego de San Pedro's *Tractado de Amores*, as well as the conception of love that dominates it, derive principally from the same source as the poetry of the *cancioneros*, with which it has more in common than with already existing forms of fiction. Verse is used

---

[11] Triangular Desire," p. 12, in *Deceit, Desire, and the Novel*.

in various ways in the story itself, as devices on shields, as inscriptions, as a song, and poems are interpolated in the work.[12]

The idealized concept of love found in the work stems from the courtly love tradition. What bothers both Regula Langbehn-Rohland and Keith Whinnom is that this concept of love is not sustained: Arnalte's lofty speeches are coupled with actions which are intended to win Lucenda, actions which seem to these critics to be ridiculous. The first to comment on this, Langbehn-Rohland, asserts that certain episodes make Arnalte look like an inept lover and a comic figure (p. 128). Keith Whinnom agrees that the behavior is an absurd contrast to Arnalte's speeches, but he argues that we must be careful in what we label as humorous since some of these episodes—such as disguising himself as a woman or offering himself as a husband for Lucenda after killing the one she had—are well-known literary devices. The humor is not found in any one episode but, as stated before, in the general contrast between word and deed:

> ¿Qué será lo que provoca a risa en *Arnalte*? Creo que la Dra. Langbehn-Rohland se ha acercado a la solución al escribir que ve un contraste absurdo y realmente cómico entre la conducta de Arnalte y los altos ideales que expone, así como entre los prosaicos detalles de algunos trozos de la narrativa y el alto estilo en que son descritos. Lo absurdo de esta novelita estriba en tales disonancias, pero queda por demostrar que San Pedro las notase, por lo menos en la época en que las escribió. (pp. 58-59)

As the lofty speeches have literary antecedents, so do the actions of Arnalte. The Ovidian tale is not a graceful love story: "Se ha dicho repetidas veces que la *Ars* ovidiana celebra no el amor sino la técnica de la seducción" (*AL*, p. 59). This combination of the spiritual and physical sides of love creates a tension within the work. It is not just a problem for the reader that Arnalte's theorizing does not match his means of carrying the theories out: it is a problem for Arnalte, an irresolvable paradox between the theoretical and the practical. I intend to prove in this analysis that San Pedro deliberately created a work of tensions in order to illustrate the impossibility of following the code of courtly love or, as it were, the type of frustrated love found in the *cancionero* poetry, when put to the test by an ordinary lover.

That the story is set in Thebes endows it with authority. Just as Rodríguez del Padrón used France and Macías to create the legend of

---

[12] "Love and Honour," p. 253.

Ardanlier and Liessa in order to provide worthy lovers for his native Galicia, San Pedro legitimizes his work by setting it in Greece. The appeal to authorities by medieval authors is certainly a commonplace. Often this is accomplished by citing several authors in true or invented quotations, and establishing the present story in the good company of these authorities. San Pedro does this not by referring to specific authorities, but by the subtle means of situating *Arnalte y Lucenda* in the land of legendary heroes. His predilection for the Greek setting is shown again in the situating of *Cárcel de Amor* in Macedonia. Furthermore, in *Sermón*, San Pedro's love guide to the ladies, which follows rules for preachers, the only *exemplum* given outside his own love rhetoric is the story of Pyramus and Thisbe.

*Arnalte y Lucenda* demonstrates a Christian dilemma of contemporary love. Love service, the exaltation of the lady and submission of the male lover, was blasphemous according to Church doctrine.[13] However, Arnalte's lofty speeches of love service are shown to be secondary to his actions, intended to bring about Lucenda's capitulation. Therefore, it is not a story of love service in the strictest sense. In fact, when, halfway through the story, Lucenda confesses her love for Arnalte, we see that the intention of the hero has not been the willingness, the necessity, to serve at all, but a calculated effort to induce a real response.

This brings into question the notion of the theoretical side of love and the practical side. The theory—which can be termed love service or courtly love—thrived in the poetry of the fifteenth century. The *topoi*, among them love as a living death, love as pain, pain as the joy of lovers, are not necessarily the historical reality. One could envision, however, a lover like Arnalte—exposed to and believing in the theory: the graceful elegance of the courtly lyric defining the nature of love. One could envision a person simply in love with the idea of being in love, much as the Tristan described by Denis de Rougemont.[14] And that is what we have in the figure of Arnalte: a lover who would be the model courtly hero but for his actions, which betray this pose.

Arnalte is not evil, although some demonic imagery does surround

---

[13] In his introduction to *Cárcel de Amor*, Keith Whinnom makes the point that the fifteenth-century authors conveniently ignored church theology when dealing with courtly love, pp. 38-39.

[14] *Love in the Western World*, trans. Montgomery Belgion (1956; rpt. New York: Harper and Row, 1974); see especially chapter 8, "The Love of Love," pp. 38-42.

him, as we will see later. If anything, he is pathetic since he behaves, at times, in a comic manner. He gains the reader's sympathy not simply because his actions make him seem real or comic, but because they are juxtaposed with his speeches which ring with sincerity. He does not appear to us to be the sly deceiver of women, using words and wiles to seduce. He is taken in by his own words and, no doubt, sees nothing incongruous in combining lofty speeches with a poke through Lucenda's garbage for remnants of his letter to her.

As we have seen in *Siervo libre de amor*, courtly love leads to frustration (e. g. Siervo) and physical love is somehow connected with violent death (Liessa, Ardanlier). In *Arnalte y Lucenda*, this combination of frustrated and physical love occurs through the concept of the double in literature, and the motif of *soledad*, which is present until Lucenda responds favorably to Arnalte, thereby recognizing the love. No sooner does Lucenda reciprocate than a new strain appears—signs, omens of unhappiness, which cause Arnalte to return to Thebes. He finds that Lucenda has wed his friend Elierso, news which sparks in Arnalte such a jealousy that he vows to kill Elierso. This kind of violence, the result of jealousy, could not have occurred without two prior events--the imitation of Arnalte by Elierso and the acceptance by Lucenda, however slight, of Arnalte's love. Without Lucenda's confession of love, Arnalte would not have had justifiable cause to see her subsequent marriage to another as his own great loss. Before, her love was merely a hope; on becoming a reality it opened a new, destructive, dimension: jealousy. Unfortunately for Arnalte, he opened the door to jealousy. Elierso was completely unaware of Arnalte's feelings for Lucenda until Arnalte pleaded with him to act as intermediary. However, unbeknownst to Arnalte, it was this action that initiated Elierso's imitative behavior.

What we can term the events of pre-reciprocity—specifically, Arnalte's letters and his private laments—lead only to *soledad* in its various definitions. The overt pursuit of Lucenda—the ambush in the church, the sending of his sister Belisa to plead his cause—leads to Lucenda's acquiescence and the subsequent violence.

Vossler's definitive study on *soledad* in Castilian literature provides many examples of the word's usage.[15] *Soledad* took on the meanings of

---

[15] Karl Vossler, *La soledad en la poesía española*, trans. José Miguel Sacristán (Madrid: Revista de Occidente, 1941). See especially "La palabra soledad," pp. 11-27.

nostalgia, melancholy, and sadness, especially in fifteenth-century *cancionero* poetry, while retaining its simple meaning of physical solitude. In this poem by the poet identified only as Guevara, *soledad* appears three times in slight variants:

> Ví las sierras temerosas
> de mortal sombra cubiertas
> las aves roncas, quexosas
> pronunciando soledad
> con sus bozes congoxosas.
> Soledad de vuestra vista
> hay solo quanto he visto,
> vuestro gesto que conquisto
> no sé bien que me resista...
> Que vos soys la soledad
> deste siglo do' stó sólo,
> y del bien que digo, solo
> vuestro gesto es la bondad...[16]

It is generally conceded that *soledad* as a complex concept took root in the middle of the sixteenth century and flourished in the seventeenth with the likes of Lope de Vega and Góngora. With the works of these authors came the notion of *soledad* as a state of mind, as a feeling of alienation, and, in its prime, as the result of one's knowledge of the world and one's place outside its artifice.[17]

Diego de San Pedro uses the word *soledad* sixteen times in *Arnalte y Lucenda*.[18] Admittedly his use of *soledad* does not attain the heights reached by the Baroque authors, but we are speaking of an author who came at least one hundred years before these artists. What is important is that the frequency of its appearance in *Arnalte y Lucenda* suggests that

[16] *Cancionero general de Hernando del Castillo*, ed. José Antonio de Balenchana, Sociedad de Bibliófilos Españoles, 21 (Madrid: 1882), I, poem 232.

[17] The concept of *soledad* appears in Rodríguez del Padrón's *Siervo libre de amor*: the second part of the work is entitled "solitaria e dolorosa contemplaçión," in which Siervo retires to the "templo de la grand soledat."

[18] It does not seem to be a word used indiscriminately by San Pedro. *Soledad* appears only twice in *Cárcel de Amor*. The first is the Auctor's narration: "Érale [a Leriano] la conpañía aborrecible y la soledad agradable," the second in the letter from the Queen to Laureola, her daughter: "Beviré en soledad de ti y en conpañía de los dolores que en tu lugar me dexas, los cuales, de conpasión, viéndome quedar sola, por aconpañadores me diste." *Obras completas*, II: *Cárcel de Amor*, ed. Keith Whinnom, pp. 98, 135. Both Whinnom, p. 135, and Vossler, p. 17, have noted the double meaning in the latter quotation of the word *soledad*.

it is intentionally used as a motif. San Pedro was aware by the early 1480's of *soledad* as a concept to be explored. In order to demonstrate the range of instances in which it appears, here are the sentences containing the word:

El Auctor: "...halléme en un grand desierto, el cual de estraña soledad y temeroso espanto era poblado." (p. 89)

"Y como allí soledad sobrase, pasión no faltava, y de verme en necessidad tan estrecha no savía qué remedio me diese." (p. 89)

Arnalte: "Y como ya en el final aposentamiento su padre fuese puesto, e ella, dexándolo en él, al suyo se fuese, enmudescido, sin más detenerme, fui la soledad a buscar, para que ella e mis pensamientos compaña me fiziesen." (p. 102)

"Y como ya a la casa de Lucenda ido fuese [the messenger], ofrecióle el tiempo el aparejo qu'él quería y yo deseava; e cuando la vido donde soledad sola conpaña le fiziesse, suplicóle mi carta quisiesse recevir." (p. 105)

"...a ella me llegué; y como de mi engaño sin sospecha estuviese, con mi llegada no se alteró; y como la soledad lugar me diese, comencé a dezirle ansí." (p. 106)

"E si el sufrimiento de padescer se cansare, llama el seso; y si él no te valiere, a la razón requiere; e si todos te dexaren, tu soledad llora, e al morir las puertas abiertas ten; que cuando no pensares, en él el remedio que el seso y la razon te negaron hallarás." (p. 111)

"Y como el rey me viese, después de mi vida preguntarme, que quisiese justar me mandó, porque él y muchos cavalleros de su corte en justar entendian; y aunque mis exercicios más dispuestos para soledad que para fiestas aparejados estoviesen, por su mandado cumplir, mi voluntad esforcé, deziéndole que pues su Alteza lo mandava, que yo lo quería." (pp. 111-12)

E como la hora del momear llegada fuese, y salidos los momos a la sala, cada uno con la dama que servía començó a dançar. Allí de mi dicha me quexé, y de mi soledad más me dolí en verme de sus riquezas tan pobre." (p. 113)

"Pero el poder y el saber, seyendo tuyos, de ser míos dexaron, y porque con quien remediarme no hallase, en gran soledad me pusieron." (p. 114)

"E como a sus mandamientos el amor tan sometido me toviese, con todas sus enponçonosas plagas ofendido me tiene; y como sus combates son tan rezios y tan pequeña mi fuerça, hanme en estrecho mortal puesto; y como sus ofensas son tan muchas e mis defendimientos tan pocos, aquellas gentese de quien valerme solía, haziéndome traición, cada cual por su parte se yendo, hanme en grand soledad dexado. Negóme el esperança; huyóme el remedio; dexóme la razón; el seso no quiso valerme." (p. 121)

Belisa: "Pues si a muerte por su vida [Arnalte's] debo ponerme, tu lo conosces e sabes, que aun tanto por la soledad mía como por la salud suya debo fazerlo; porque tú sabes bien que la corruta pestilencia pasada de nuestros padres y parientes nos dexó solos." (pp. 125-26)

"Estiende tu galardón, pues no encoxas por él tu virtud; en cual él irá piensa, y en cual yo quedaré contempla; su perdición mira; mi soledad no olvides; de su dolor faz memoria;... y no dañes a ti ni destruyas a él ni atormentes a mí." (p. 130)

Arnalte: "Y porque no pienses que cosa que te dañase pedirte podría, no te pido que en lugar que soledad guarde el secreto mefables, mas en parte que la remediadora y hermana mía medianera sea." (p. 135)

Belisa: "Y si esto no te costriñe, que te acuerdes de mi soledad te encomiendo. Bien sabes tú que mi honra por la tuya es conserbada;... bien sabes tú que la muerte de nuestros padres y parientes me fizo sola. Pero contigo nunca de soledad me quexé; antes muy acompañada siempre me vi." (p. 166)

Arnalte: "La fazienda desde hoy la fago tuya; y no pienses tú en mí poner tal falta para que en la soledad tan grande dexado te hoviese, que ya quien te faga compañía tengo buscado." (p. 168)

The first use of the word (p. 89) is by the narrator and is accompanied by the adjective *estraña*. As it turns out, this is important for the ending since Arnalte relates the tale to the narrator and has elected to spend the rest of his days in the place where the narrator begins his narration, in the place of *estraña soledad*. But the exact nature of the *estraña soledad* and the reason for it are not known until the end.

In Arnalte's first speech to the narrator he tells him that, after seeing Lucenda at her father's funeral, he sought *soledad* (p. 102), a simple solitude. Apparently deciding that a contemplative solitude is not satisfying enough, he embarks on the road to win Lucenda's favor. His page is sent with a letter for Lucenda. When the page sees her in *soledad* (p. 105), meaning, quite simply, that no one else was around at the moment, he attempts to pass along the letter.

The next appearance of *soledad* (p. 106) comes at the time of Arnalte's disguise as a woman, hoping for a secret moment with Lucenda in church. Here, *soledad* is, again, an opportune moment of approach, but since he is hidden, it also suggests darkness, hidden recesses, and possibly, something illicit.

When Lucenda rejects him, and after he has spent some time singing under her window, Arnalte launches into a long soliloquy, at the end of which *soledad* is employed as a mental state, as the result of the departure of one's reason:

E si el sufrimiento de padescer se cansare, llama
el seso; y si él no te valiere, a la razón requiere;
e si todos te dexaren, tu soledad llora,
e al morir las puertas abiertas ten... (p. 111)

The similarity of this thought to a poem by Juan Agraz in the *Cancionero de Palacio* is striking:

Pensaría villanía,
mi senyora, quien pensase
que tu coraçón amasse
quien servido no t'avía
e dexar quien te servía.

Senyora, tu soledat
más la siento que la mía
no te vença tal porfía
por que falses lealtat... [19]

However, the main difference is that Arnalte's lament is for himself and his own *soledad*, due to the departure of abstractions such as reason and will. Juan Agraz uses a double meaning to refer to the love service.

Arnalte visits the King and finds that he is to be included in a joust and a mumming. This scene is the occasion of two mentions of *soledad*. In fact, it is used as a juxtaposition of meaning. While alone with the King, he thinks: "mis exercicios [están] más dispuestos para soledad que para fiestas" (p. 112). In this case, there is nothing profound about the meaning of *soledad*, which here simply refers to being alone. But a few paragraphs later, when he sees the mummers dancing with the ladies and he is with Lucenda, he laments his lot: "Allí de mi dicha me quexé, y de mi soledad más me dolí en verme de sus riquezas tan pobre" (p. 113). *Soledad* here, is, naturally, being without a lady to serve, but it represents also deprivation, emptiness, not the state of being alone. One can experience *soledad*, therefore, even in the midst of a crowd.

---

[19] *El cancionero de Palacio (manuscrito n.º 594)*, ed. Francisca Vendrell de Millás (Barcelona: CSIC, 1945), poem 246, pp. 311-12. This poem was mentioned by Vossler, p. 17, although quoted from another source, as an example of how, occasionally, a fifteenth-century poet could employ *soledad* in a double meaning; here, nostalgia for the lady and actual aloneness on the part of the poet.

This is reinforced immediately after the mumming when Arnalte writes a letter in which he laments, once again, his present state. He attributes his sense of *soledad* (p. 114) to the fact that power and knowledge have left him and now belong only to Lucenda.

Searching for a solution, Arnalte writes to Elierso, telling him of his desertion by his men, symbolically expressing what he states soon after, that reason, hope and remedy for his ills have all deserted him, leaving him "en grand soledad" (p. 121). The description harks back to the soliloquy in which he enumerated his resources, knowing that they might be depleted soon after. Here, at the point of despair, we see that indeed they have been.

Belisa, Arnalte's sister, is the next to mention *soledad* (pp. 125-26). For her, it is being without any family. She tells Lucenda, in effect, that she would rather die than be left with no family, her parents already having died from the plague. In this context *soledad* is broadened to mean not only lovers, but kin. When Belisa continues in her efforts to convince Lucenda, she reaffirms *soledad* on the level of kinship: "su perdicion mira, mi soledad no olvides" (p. 130). The idea of *soledad* as suggesting something illicit reappears as Arnalte begs Lucenda that they meet, not "en lugar que soledad guarde el secreto" (p. 135), but where Belisa can be the intercessor.

*Soledad* is then forgotten until after Arnalte has lost all hope of winning Lucenda and has completed his long poem to the Virgin Mary, hoping that she will bestow consolation. He announces his intention to withdraw from court society and Belisa pleads with him to reconsider, citing again her *soledad* (p. 166). Arnalte makes the final mention of *soledad*. He tells his sister that he has not left her in "la soledad tan grande" (p. 168), because he has already found a lifetime companion for her in the form of a husband.

Since Arnalte makes good his intention to leave society, the text is circular. We are brought back to the present where the narrator is hearing Arnalte's tale, and we recall that it takes place in the desert dominated by *estraña soledad* (p. 89). Why is it *estraña soledad*? The answer lies in the examination of the concept of *soledad* as it appears in this work.

Before Lucenda acquiesces and admits to loving Arnalte (or, at least, declaring that he is the victor), *soledad* appears as a natural consequence of desire and love service. It is a matter of choice inasmuch as Arnalte seeks solitude in order to reflect. As the passion becomes more consuming and frustrating, *soledad* for Arnalte has a double meaning. There is seclusion, withdrawal by choice (he states that he prefers to be alone rather than take part in court activities). And there is *soledad* which refers to the state of mind, the emptiness caused by reason's desertion. Love's debilitating nature is demonstrated by Arnalte's melancholy, resulting in his failing health. He never ceases to calculate ways to pursue Lucenda actively. However, when she finally confesses her love, he takes off for a retreat outside Thebes in order to recover. His need to pursue her abated, Arnalte behaves somewhat like Calisto, whom we see lost some interest in Melibea once she acquiesced. *Soledad* is never mentioned in this section of voluntary retreat, even though it would seem natural to do so, but is replaced by a very real, human double which sparks violence. Arnalte is plagued by signs that all is not well and returns to Thebes to find Lucenda married to his friend Elierso. He is driven to kill Elierso: violence has sprung from jealousy. And, because Lucenda, widowed, rejects his offer of marriage, Arnalte has no choice but withdrawal from society. It is not because he loved her and suffered the *soledad* which results from love, but because he abandons the ideal of pining away in secrecy and pursued love in an active or physical way. This kind of pursuit, as we have seen time and again, leads without fail to violence. In this case, violence resulted from the jealousy which comes from a sense of having lost one's own property.

The conclusion to Arnalte's love quest is a life-death in a desert of *estraña soledad: estraña* because it is not the spiritual *soledad* of the contemplative lover, but that of one who has known violence and shame.

The concept of *soledad* functions as an independent construct in *Arnalte y Lucenda*, that is to say, it is a motif independent of strict association with any one character. However, at certain points, it intersects another construct, that of the doubling of the protagonist through the employment of his sister as intermediary. Not every go-between functions as Belisa does: she is a blood relative, for one, and she pleads with Lucenda, not simply for Arnalte's case, but for her own heart, which she claims is inextricably bound to Arnalte's.

The double, a prominent figure in romance, appears in varied forms: twin, mirror image, antithetical character (often referred to as demonic double), or, simply, a character which embodies one or two traits recognizable as characteristic of another.[20] Much has been made

[20] In *A Psychoanalytic Study of the Double in Literature* (Detroit: Wayne State University Press, 1970), Robert Rogers discusses the term "doubling" and reminds us that it does not necessarily refer to exact duplication, but can refer to duplication, division, fragmentation, and decomposition, pp. 1-17.

of the demonic double, no doubt because the fundamental conflict plaguing mankind is that of good and evil.[21]

Critics have concentrated on medieval epistolary composition for the understanding of *Arnalte y Lucenda*, but not enough attention has been given to the work as romance.[22] The reason for this neglect is that critics have tended to sum up the plot in terms of the letters and dialogue, whereas the fact is, some of the most intriguing plot developments, to say nothing of the imagery normally associated with romance, occur during Arnalte's narration, leading into the letters and meetings.

Belisa does not appear in *Arnalte y Lucenda* until Arnalte has established himself as a dark figure of sorts, having already fallen in love at a funeral; sent his page to Lucenda; hidden himself, disguised as a woman, in a church; sung at night outside her house; confronted the King and taken part in a joust and mumming. Arnalte's description of Belisa establishes her as having a strong link to him: "Y como una hermana mía, que Belisa se llamava, estraño amor me toviese, de mi dolor mucho se doliendo, para mi un dia se vino...E como estremo amor muy conformes nuestras voluntades toviese, al son de sus lágrimas mis ojos dançaban" (pp. 116-17). Belisa declares her loyalty and feeling of oneness with her brother: "Tus males y los míos un coraçón atormientan" (p. 117). Arnalte refuses to confide in her: "E porque tú toda alegre y yo todo triste vivamos, te suplico que así lo concedas;...asi que pues ver tu tormento con doble pasión el mío atormenta, grand merced rescibiría que de mi cuidado te descuides" (pp. 119-20). The characters, for a time at least, retain some individuality, although the groundwork has been laid for the merging of their goals. Belisa, persistent in her efforts to discover Arnalte's loved one, decides

---

[21] For a study of the double in romance, see Northrop Frye, *The Secular Scripture: A Study of the Structure of Romance* (Cambridge, MA: Harvard University Press, 1976; rpt. 1978), pp. 108-18. René Girard studies the double in two works: *Violence and the Sacred*, especially "From Mimetic Desire to the Monstrous Double," pp. 143-68, and *Deceit, Desire, and the Novel*. The theme of the double runs throughout this critical work, but can be found especially in "Triangular Desire," pp. 1-52, and "Men Become Gods in the Eyes of Each Other," pp. 53-82.

[22] Two critics in particular have been interested in the question of epistolary composition, Keith Whinnom (pp. 60-63), and E. Michael Gerli. While this was being prepared, Professor Gerli kindly showed me a typescript of his then forthcoming book on sentimental romance, in which he concentrates heavily on the rules of *dictamen* for his interpretation of *Arnalte y Lucenda*.

that it is Lucenda, whom she knows well. Unlike Arnalte, who deals in roundabout ways of approaching Lucenda, Belisa goes directly to her and speaks up. Now, part of the explanation is that Belisa is a woman and Lucenda's friend, so she is able to approach her. However, the action does serve as contrast to Arnalte's nocturnal activities. Also, Belisa, as a woman, can be a double of Arnalte without actually representing competition for Lucenda, which might be the case were she a man.

At this meeting between Lucenda and Belisa, the first mentioned in the narrative, occurs the mention of *soledad* linked to lineage. Lucenda responds negatively to Belisa's pleas on Arnalte's behalf so Belisa tries again, this time applying the burden of guilt for two lives lost: "Pues si tú tal consientes, de su destierro y mi muerte serás causa...Podrás, si lo fazes, alabarte que con un amén salvaste dos vidas" (pp. 129-30). Lucenda answers almost as if speaking to a lover:

> "El consejo para engañarme no fue ligero, pues podré yo llamarme de tu fuerça forçada y no de mi voluntad vencida; ... y tanto amor te tengo que quiero, porque ganes tú, perder yo; ... E ruégote que el prescio de mi sí nunca desprecies; porque es regla general por natural tenida, que todas las cosas cuando haver no se pueden son estimadas, y después de havidas suelen en menosprecio venir" (p. 131).

Up until this point Belisa's entreaties have been straightforward enough, although it can be considered unfair to place a double burden of guilt on the hesitant lover. Belisa's wishes are indistinguishable from Arnalte's. However, Arnalte is not satisfied with Lucenda's letters and engages Belisa in one of his secret rendezvous. Belisa is no longer a double but an unwilling accomplice and intermediary, begging Lucenda to meet with Arnalte.

After the meeting it is Belisa's idea that Arnalte recover from his love sickness in their country retreat. From then until the end of the story, Belisa is not a double, although she does bring Arnalte confirmation of Lucenda's wedding and, later, tries to speak to Lucenda who has entered the convent. When she confronts Arnalte at the end of the tale, it is not as his double in desire, nor as the intermediary between two lovers, but as mediator between society and the soon-to-be exile. Although the relationship of lineage and *soledad* is brought up again, the characters have split, leaving us with two people, one who will leave society and one who will marry and remain a part of the court.

Belisa and Arnalte merge in a sense and then are separated at the

end. Arnalte and Elierso are friends-turned-rivals and the result is
Elierso's death. As in happier romances, such as Heliodorus' *Aethiopian
History* and Chrétien de Troyes' *Yvain*, to name two very diverse
examples, the plot moves towards the joining of the hero and the
heroine, usually expressed by a harmonious community scene—banquet, wedding, or trial resolved in favor of the protagonists. *Arnalte y
Lucenda*, the actual narration of Arnalte that is, progresses from a
somber community scene—Lucenda's father's funeral—during which
Arnalte falls in love with Lucenda, to the ending which results not
just in Arnalte's self-imposed exile but in Belisa's marriage.

If Belisa can, in effect, be seen as a double or alter ego of Arnalte,
what is the purpose? It points out the paths open to the protagonist—
involvement with Lucenda notwithstanding. As Denis de Rougemont
sums up: "The Middle Ages had two rival moral systems—one upheld
by Christianized society, the other the product of heretical courtesy"
(p. 275). The Christianized society pointed to marriage, not love
service, as the only viable love relationship between men and women.
In a work designed to demonstrate the tensions of a Christian society
dominated by the ideas of *cancionero* poetry, Arnalte's story is an
*exemplum*.

Belisa, although she helped Arnalte, did so because of her love for
him, which is shown almost as a merging of her goals and needs into
his. But this was not her love affair, it was Arnalte's. Belisa represents
the light, or open action, Arnalte the darkness, which reflects a
fundamental idea in the world view of man. Denis de Rougemont says:

> "From India to the shore of the Atlantic, though in the most varied
> forms, there is expressed the same mystery of Day and Night and
> the same mystery of the fatal struggle going on between them
> inside men's breasts. There is a god of uncreated and timeless Light,
> and there is a god of Darkness, the author of evil, who holds sway
> over all visible creation" (p. 63).

Woman represents both light and dark, which was Christianized as
the Eve-Mary antithesis. San Pedro does not neglect this idea, although his suggestion of it is subtle. He has been criticized for what
looks like a clumsy addition of the poetic sorrows of Our Lady to a
prose narrative. The criticism of style may be valid, but at least we
can detect a reason for its inclusion: it recalls that there is one other
woman, in addition to Isabel la Católica—named in the earlier poem
of the work—who is worthy of praise and devotion—Mary. In fact,
Eve is briefly mentioned in the poem: "¡O hijo, que tanto es llena / de

dolor esta desculpa, / pues para todos es buena, / yo rescibiré la pena / pues Eva causó la culpa!" (p. 159).

At the end of *Arnalte y Lucenda*, Belisa's sense of companionship, her salvation from *soledad*, arises out of a court-approved marriage, not resulting from a passionate love affair. Arnalte's fate is exile, thereby eliminating the likelihood of a similar companionship.

*Arnalte y Lucenda* is composed of various triangular relationships:

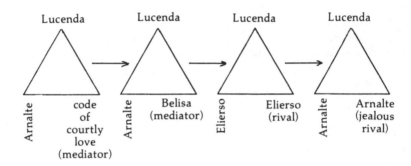

The first two triangles can be understood in terms of the above analysis of Arnalte's combination of courtly conduct and techniques of pursuit, and Belisa's role as the intermediary/double of Arnalte. At the point when Arnalte retires to the country at Belisa's urging, her role as his double ends and Elierso's begins. Technically, Elierso's role as rival began earlier and is completely the fault of Arnalte. Having pleaded with Elierso to aid him in his pursuit of Lucenda, Arnalte unwittingly initiates a relationship of triangular desire. That Elierso identifies himself with Arnalte is proven in the following letter, and is stated in a manner similar to one of Belisa's own remarks about her relationship with Arnalte: "Dízesme que la hermosura de Lucenda tu vida destruye; tu cuidado y el mío una causa los causa; y si ella tu bien adolesce, mi salud atormenta. Mas porque diversidad en tu voluntad y en la mía no se conosca, desde hoy de tal cuidado me descuido" (p. 123). Nothing more is heard from Elierso until Arnalte learns that he and Lucenda are married. What is interesting here is the reversal of the subject (Arnalte) and the rival (Elierso) with regard to the object (Lucenda), and the additional aspect that Elierso claims to have done Arnalte a favor. Elierso claims that his love for Arnalte, not his desire for Lucenda, led him to this act:

Yo supe mejor guardar el amistad que tú conservarla, y si en plaça no me afrontaras, de mi desculpa en secreto satisfecho fueras, la cual saviendo, más por cierto que por engañoso me juzgaras, porque más por remedio tuyo que por provecho mío a Lucenda por muger resciví, creyendo que su casamiento para en tus males atajo sería. (p. 145)

Arnalte is overcome with jealousy and, even though it seemed that his own interest in Lucenda had abated somewhat, new intensity of feeling is aroused. He challenges Elierso to a duel and kills him. This consequence is in keeping with my contention that in the sentimental romances physical love is always connected with violence. We can assume that Elierso and Lucenda consummated their marriage. Even though neither of the original lovers—Arnalte and Lucenda—dies in this work, it is similar to the other sentimental romances of violent love in that the person who does pursue and achieve a physical relationship with a lover will die, in this case, Elierso, the third point of the triangle. That is not to say that marriage itself is wrong. Indeed, the ending, Belisa's marriage to a gentleman, is clearly a favorable action. Elierso was deceiving himself consciously or unconsciously in his self-proclaimed altruistic motive for marrying Lucenda. No doubt he, too, was caught in desire's web and paid the penalty exacted in these romances.

### Conclusion

What all this suggests, therefore, is the purpose behind the tensions: the comic acts juxtaposed with lofty speeches; the actions intended to provoke Lucenda's acquiescence and the rhetorical laments associated with *cancionero* and troubadour poetry; the concept of *soledad*, now referring to contemplative solitude, now to lurking in the darkness; the tensions presented by the ever-changing triangular relationships, and, finally, the tension created by the merging of Arnalte and Belisa, by Elierso's mimetic desire, and the varied results of these actions—marriage for one person, exile for another, and death for the third. In generalizing the differences between San Pedro's works and those of Flores, Pamela Waley says:

The novels of Diego de San Pedro are concerned with the idealized conception of love that belongs to the realm of poetry; those of Juan de Flores derive largely from the fiction of Boccaccio, and in the main discuss love as observed behaviour between men and women. (p. 263)

She is partly right; San Pedro is concerned with *cancionero*-type love but not to the exclusion of reality, at least not in *Arnalte y Lucenda*. *Arnalte y Lucenda* views this type of love precisely through the observed behavior of one lover who tries, on the one hand, to reconcile active pursuit with solitary suffering and, on the other hand, to make amends through newfound solitude in the desert, for what occurred through jealousy: Elierso's death and Lucenda's retirement from the world.

*Love Service, the Active Narrator, and the Jealous Rival in "Cárcel de Amor"*

*Cárcel de Amor* is a study of desire as the impulse of a chain of events, as it is in *Grisel y Mirabella*, and as triangular desire in action.

In terms of triangular relationships, *Cárcel de Amor* is divided into three major phases of comparable narrative length. In the background of the work there is an implied mediator in the form of a role model— the code of courtly love—to which Leriano is adhering when he is first spotted by the narrator. Leriano implores El Auctor, the narrator, to become the mediator between Laureola and himself. Later, in the second phase of the work, the emphasis shifts from the narrator as mediator to the actions of Persio, the jealous rival, and we witness, along with the narrator, triangular desire in action. When this is resolved, Leriano returns to the condition he was in when the story opened: a prisoner of love. *Cárcel de Amor* begins with an allegorical portrayal of Desire as a Wild Man who is dragging the unfortunate prisoner of love, Leriano, through the dark mountain area. The story is an eyewitness account by the narrator—El Auctor—who follows the two through the woods. The jailor tells the narrator that his name is Deseo and his role is to cause love and then to burn the victims with it. At this point, Deseo leaves the narrator behind and continues on his way with Leriano. The narrator spends a fearful night in the woods. When morning arrives, he sees the edifice: the "Cárcel de Amor."

Upon approaching and entering it, El Auctor encounters Leriano seated in a chair of fire. Leriano explains why he is there and that Deseo and the others present, Razón, Voluntad, Memoria, and Entendimiento, are part of himself. There follows an interpretation of that which makes up man's faculties. Leriano tells El Auctor that the first person one encounters is Deseo, "el cual a todas tristezas abre la puerta" (p. 90). After interpreting the various allegorical figures, Leriano makes his request that El Auctor tell Laureola of what he has seen and heard.

*Cárcel de Amor* is an odd combination of unrealistic and realistic narration. Upon hearing Leriano's problem, El Auctor responds immediately with the pragmatic concern that, as a foreigner, he is hampered by a language problem, and a social one—that Laureola is his social superior—and that the gravity of the situation exceeds his talents as a mediator.

He is persuaded to go, however, and does so. He worms his way into court life until he feels that he knows Laureola well enough to bring up Leriano's plight. El Auctor asks Laureola for some kind of alleviation of Leriano's suffering, and, although he does not specify what it is Laureola can do, he says: "No sé qué escusa pongas para no remediallo, si no crees que matar es virtud; no te suplica que le hagas otro bien sino que te pese de su mal, que cosa grave para ti no creas que te la pidiría, que por mejor havrá el penar que serte a ti causa de pena" (p. 95).

Laureola indignantly responds with what may be the only intentional humor she shows in the story, and chastizes El Auctor for his gall in questioning her kindness and suggesting her culpability in Leriano's plight:

> Si como eres d'España fueras de Macedonia, tu razonamiento y tu vida acabaran a un tienpo; ... porque no solamente por el atrevimiento devías morir, mas por la ofensa que a mi bondad heziste, en la cual posiste dubda; ... Avísote, aunque seas estraño en la nación, que serás natural en la sepoltura. (p. 96)

As an interpreter of emotions, El Auctor does not succeed. He feels, in spite of his initial inability to draw out of Laureola any compassion for Leriano, that she, in fact, does care for him. Encouraged by this interpretation of the interview, El Auctor returns to Leriano and suggests that he write to Laureola.

In his letter to Laureola, Leriano recognizes love as a chain:

> Podrás dezir que cómo pensé escrevirte; no te maravilles, que tu hermosura causó el afición, y el afición el deseo, y el deseo la pena, y la pena el atrevimiento, y si porque lo hize te pareciere que merezco muerte, mándamela dar, que muy mejor es morir por tu causa que bevir sin tu esperança. (p. 99)

Laureola accepts the letter, but explains her reservations: women must, above all else, retain their honor, their good reputation. Therefore, much as she would like to help the unfortunate Leriano, she cannot risk the loss of her honor.

Leriano sees no recourse but death, so he writes to Laureola, and El Auctor delivers the letter. Stunned by this turn of events and overwhelmed by guilt, Laureola responds in a letter, but warns:

Por Dios te pido que enbuelvas mi carta en tu fe, porque si es tan cierta como confiesas, no se te pierda ni de nadie pueda ser vista; que quien viese lo que te escrivo pensaría que te amo, y creería que mis razones antes eran dichas por disimulación de la verdad que por la verdad. Lo cual es al revés, que por cierto más las digo, como ya he dicho, con intención piadosa que con voluntad enamorada. (p. 110)

El Auctor returns to the countryside where Leriano awaits. Upon receiving the letter, Leriano is overjoyed:

Y entretanto que la leía todos los que levava comigo procuravan su salud: Alegría le alegrava el coraçón, Descanso le consolava el alma, Esperança le bolvía el sentido, Contentamiento le aclarava la vista, Holgança le restituía la fuerça, Plazer le abivava el entendimiento; y en tal manera lo trataron que cuando lo que Laureola le escrivió acabó de leer, estava tan sano como si ninguna pasión huviera tenido. (pp. 112-13)

There is a similarity between Leriano's case and those of Arnalte and Calisto. Arnalte, when he finally receives Lucenda's verbal declaration of affection, retires to the country in order to recover from his ardor. The point is that the ardent pursuit abates when some sign of reciprocity is given. Calisto, as is commonly known, cannot live without the love of Melibea, but his ardor cools noticeably when Melibea gives in to his sexual advances.[23]

El Auctor persuades Leriano to return to the court. What has, throughout this first phase of *Cárcel de Amor*, been a dichotomy of court and country, and the tensions which exist between the expectations of love in those two places, changes to the tensions within a single place, the court, which arise from the jealousy associated with love.

Leriano and Laureola greet each other while the self-satisfied narrator looks on. However, he is not alone in viewing the arrival of Leriano:

---

[23] In the Middle Ages, this was considered to be, apparently, a more radical cure. As Aldo D. Scaglione, *Nature and Love in the Late Middle Ages* (Berkeley: University of California Press, 1963), explains: "In desperate cases, doctors were even advised to favor the meeting of the lover with the object of his passion, for this would end his infatuation and cure him... This 'scientific' naïveté of curing the lover by pandering for him is, after all, not too surprising (though Boccaccio, himself no physician, simply by his psychological intuition could have easily perceived the alleged 'remedy' of intercourse as perhaps the most assured way to strengthen and perpetuate the disease)," p. 61.

Y puesto que de las mudanças dellos ninguno toviese noticia por la poca sospecha que de su pendencia havía, Persio, hijo del señor de Gavia, miró en ellas trayendo el mismo pensamiento que Leriano traía; y como las sospechas celosas escudriñan las cosas secretas, tanto miró de allí adelante las hablas y señales dél que dio crédito a lo que sospechava, y no solamente dio fe a lo que veía, que no era nada, mas a lo que imaginava, que era el todo. (p. 113)

Persio informs the King, Laureola's father, of what he believes to have been the secret affair between Laureola and Leriano. El Auctor does not relinquish his role of mediator in this second phase of the work, but it is now secondary in importance to Persio's role as the jealous rival.

Persio and Leriano do battle in order to determine who is telling the truth. Persio's hand is cut off, indicating that God is on Leriano's side. Persio succeeds in bribing three men to lie to the King, and, in spite of the supplications of Leriano, the Cardinal, and Laureola, the King believes Persio and the three liars, and he sentences Laureola to death and Leriano to exile. Leriano and his men plot to rescue Laureola from where she is imprisoned. They set out to rescue her, there is a skirmish, Persio is killed, Laureola rescued, and is taken to Susa. The King lays siege to the town, many people on both sides are killed and, finally, one of the men who lied is trapped:

Y puesto en poder de Leriano, mandó que todas las maneras de tormento fuesen obradas en él hasta que dixese por qué levantó el testimonio; el cual sin premia ninguna confesó todo el hecho como pasó; y después que Leriano de la verdad se informó, enbióle al rey suplicándole que salvase a Laureola de culpa y que mandase justiciar aquél y a los otros que de tanto mal havién sido causa; lo cual el rey, sabido lo cierto, aceutó con alegre voluntad por la justa razón que para ello le requería; y por no detenerme en la prolixidades que en este caso pasaron, de los tres falsos hombres se hizo tal la justicia como fue la maldad. (p. 148)

Since the truth is now known, the King takes Laureola home and pardons Leriano. But, instead of rewarding him or begging his forgiveness, the King warns Leriano that he must stay away from the court until things have been smoothed over with Persio's family:

A Leriano mandóle el rey que no entrase por estonces en la corte hasta que pacificase a él y a los parientes de Persio, lo que recibió a graveza porque no podría ver a Laureola, y no podiendo hazer otra cosa, sintióle en estraña manera; y viéndose apartado della, dexadas las obras de guerra, bolvióse a las cogoxas enamoradas; y deseoso de saber en lo que Laureola estava, rogóme que le fuese a suplicar que diese alguna forma honesta para que la pudiese ver y hablar. (pp. 148-50)

Thus, the third phase of the work begins with Leriano once again consumed by passion, and the narrator sent as messenger to Laureola. Laureola, more wary than enamored, writes to Leriano that he must not contact her again because her reputation will undoubtedly suffer:

Cuando estava presa salvaste mi vida, y agora que estó libre quieres condenalla; pues tanto me quieres, antes devrías querer tu pena con mi honrra que tu remedio con mi culpa; no creas que tan sanamente biven las gentes que, sabido que te hablé, juzgasen nuestras linpias intenciones, porque tenemos tienpo tan malo, que antes se afea la bondad que se alaba la virtud. (p. 153)

Leriano despairs and falls into a mortal lovesickness. His friend Tefeo, seeing his severe condition, rages against women. Leriano rouses himself long enough to enumerate various examples of the defense of women: "Y dando comienço a la intención tomada, quiero mostrar quinze causas por que yerran los que en esta nación ponen lengua; y veinte razones por que les somos los honbres obligados; y diversos enxenplos de su bondad" (p. 156). The effort of the defense brings Leriano to the point of death. His mother arrives and, seeing her son "en ell agonía mortal" (p. 172), she faints, is revived, and commences a lamentation similar to that of Pleberio in *Celestina*:

¡O muerte, cruel enemiga, que ni perdonas los culpados ni asuelves los inocentes! Tan traidora eres, que nadie para contigo tiene defensa; amenazas para la vejez y lievas en la mocedad; a unos matas por malicia y a otros por enbidia; aunque tardas, nunca olvidas; sin ley y sin orden te riges. (p. 173)[24]

Leriano dies, but not before swallowing Laureola's letters, which have been torn to shreds and placed in a cup. The narrator relates the end of Leriano's life: "Y llegada ya la hora de su fin, puestos en mí los ojos, dixo: 'Acabados son mis males', y assí quedó su muerte en testimonio de su fe" (p. 176). El Auctor leaves after Leriano's funeral:

---

[24] The similarity between Leriano's mother's lamentation and that of Pleberio, which clearly indicates that Rojas borrows from *Cárcel*, has been demonstrated by F. Castro Guisasola, *Observaciones sobre las fuentes literarias de "La Celestina,"* Anejos de la *RFE*, 5 (Madrid: Centro de Estudios Históricos, 1924), p. 183 and by Keith Whinnom in his introduction to *Cárcel de Amor*, pp. 59-60.

Sus honrras fueron conformes a su merecimiento, las cuales aca-
badas, acordé de partirme. Por cierto con mejor voluntad caminara
para la otra vida que para esta tierra; con sospiros caminé; con
lágrimas partí; con gemidos hablé; y con tales pasatienpos llegué aquí
a Peñafiel, donde quedo besando las manos de vuestra merced. (p.
176)

The third phase of the work ends with the destructive nature of love
triumphant. The progression of the triangular relationships can be
seen in this diagram:

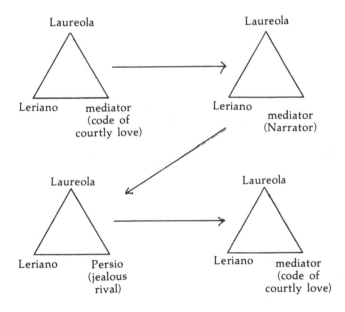

Once again, as in *Arnalte y Lucenda*, jealousy has sparked violence, a
violence which turned against the jealous person. Even though Persio
is dead and the three liars have been brought to justice, the love
relationship cannot continue. Leriano sees no recourse but suicide, the
supreme form of protest that attests to love's power. The reader is left
to wonder if justice has been served at all, since there seems to be much
talk about it, but little evidence of it.

### The Interplay of Love and Justice in "Cárcel de Amor"

Love and justice play a crucial role in the events of *Cárcel de Amor*, as
they do in *Grisel y Mirabella*. The question of justice changes according

to each phase of the work. In the first part, the narrator moves back and forth from court to country in an attempt to bring about an accord of wills between Leriano and Laureola. The country is traditionally associated with an acceptance of love, and it is from the country that Leriano sends his letters to Laureola, encouraging her to acknowledge her feelings for him.[25] Laureola, from her father's court, at first cannot admit to any feelings for Leriano, since she fears the harm it may do her reputation. The court represents an inhibition of free expression, particularly of a natural expression of love, and an overwhelming concern for one's honor, even as in the King's case, when it tends to skew justice.

Their arguments revolve around the idea of justice in love. At first, when Leriano interprets the allegory of love, he explains that four faculties must consent to this emotion: "Y por hazer de mí justa justicia preguntó por sí a cada uno si consentía que me prendiesen, porque si alguno no consentiese me absolvería de la pena" (p. 89). Entendimiento, Razón, Memoria, and Voluntad all agree to enslave Leriano. When El Auctor initially approaches Laureola, it is to tell her that she will be judged a cruel woman if she does not help alleviate Leriano's lovesickness, but will be rewarded if she does help him. Laureola responds to this suggestion with more leniency than El Auctor has shown in judging her:

> Assí que por ser estraño, no recebirás la pena que merecías, y no menos por la piedad que de mí juzgaste, comoquiera que en casos semejantes tan devida es la justicia como la clemencia, la cual en ti secutada pudiera causar dos bienes: el uno, que otros escarmentaran, y el otro que las altas mugeres fueran estimadas y tenidas segund merecen. (p. 96)

The justice Laureola refers to is a social one and not the abstract one which Leriano continues to demand. He writes to her, telling her of her obligations to his love. Laureola, concerned for her honor, tells El Auctor:

> Si pudiese remediar su mal sin amanzillar mi honrra, no con menos afición que tú lo pides yo lo haría; mas ya tú conosces cuánto las mugeres deven ser más obligadas a su fama que a su vida, la cual

---

[25] For a discussion of the notion of court and country as important elements in the sentimental romances, see Edward J. Dudley, "Court and Country: The Fusion of Two Images of Love in Juan Rodríguez' *El siervo libre de amor*," *PMLA*, 82 (1967), 117-20.

deven estimar en lo menos por razón de lo más, que es la bondad...
Pues en tus palabras con la razón te conformas ¿cómo cosa tan
injusta demandas? (p. 103)

When Leriano writes again, it is to inform Laureola of his inevitable
death should she refuse to write back to him. This time, Laureola does
write to him, but cautions: "La muerte que esperavas tú de penado,
merecía yo por culpada si en esto que hago pecase mi voluntad, lo que
cierto no es assí, que más te scrivo por redemir tu vida que por
satisfazer tu deseo" (p. 109).

Leriano returns to the court and Love has won the first round. The
court-and-country dichotomy disappears, the jealous rival appears and
along with him appear various interpretations of justice and honor.
The King relies on the word of honor of his subject, Persio, and the
system of his kingdom's laws. Leriano believes that God will make
manifest the truth in a duel between the two men: the one who is
telling the truth will be the winner. Leriano succeeds in cutting off
Persio's right hand and judges this to be sufficient proof of his and
Laureola's innocence. But here, man-made justice conflicts with natural justice:[26]

> Y como ciertos cavalleros sus parientes le [a Persio] viesen en
> estrecho de muerte, suplicaron al rey mandase echar el baston, que
> ellos le fiavan para que dél hiziese justicia si claramente se hallase
> culpado; lo cual el rey assí les otorgó; y como fuesen despartidos,
> Leriano de tan grande agravio con mucha razón se sentió, no
> podiendo pensar por qué el rey tal cosa mandase. (pp. 117-18)

Leriano begs the King's justice in recognizing the correct focus on
honor. He hopes that the King will agree to punish Persio for his
accusation:

[26] Francisco Márquez Villanueva, "*Cárcel de Amor*, novela política," in *Relecciones de literatura medieval*, Colección de Bolsillo, 54 (Seville: Publicaciones de la
Universidad de Sevilla, 1977), pp. 75-94, interprets the long interpolation of
non-amorous adventures as San Pedro's form of political protest against the
Spanish Inquisition. The discussions of clemency and justice and of the King's
inflexible attitude towards the presumed guilt of the lovers may well mask a
criticism of the political situation of the time, but does not necessarily do so.
For example, the second half of *Estoria de dos amadores* is concerned with more
than amorous adventures. The King in *Grisel y Mirabella*, who invokes the law
of Scotland against the lovers, is just as inflexible as the King in *Cárcel de Amor*.
Moreover, as I show in this chapter, the theme of justice is not restricted to
society's laws, but includes justice in love, which links the sections of the text.

Señor, las cosas de honrra deven ser claras, y si a éste perdonas, por
ruegos o por ser principal en tu reino o por lo que te plazerá, no
quedaré en los juizios de las gentes por desculpado del todo, que si
unos creyeren la verdad por razón, otros la turbarán con malicia; y
digo que en tu reino lo cierto se sepa, nunca la fama lexos lo cierto;
¿cómo sonará en los otros lo que es pasado si queda sin castigo
público? (pp. 120-21)

The King sends Leriano "a una villa suya que estava dos leguas de la
corte, llamada Susa, entretanto que acordava en el caso" (p. 121).
Persio arranges for three men to lie about the supposed affair between Leriano and Laureola, and the King believes them: "Pues
queriendo el rey que pasage la inocencia de Laureola por la traición de
los falsos testigos, acordó que fuese sentenciada por justicia" (p. 122).

El Auctor suggests various courses of action to Leriano, all of which
suggest a logical approach to solving the problem:

Lo que antes se conviene negociar es esto: yo iré a la corte y juntaré
con el cardenal de Gausa todos los cavalleros y perlados que ahí se
hallaren, el cual con voluntad alegre suplicará al rey le otorgue a
Laureola la vida; y si en esto no hallare remedio, suplicaré a la reina
que con todas las honestas y principales mugeres de su casa y cibdad
le pida la libertad de su hija, a cuyas lágrimas y petición no podrá, a
mi creer, negar piedad; y si aquí no hallo esperança, diré a Laureola
que le escriva certificándole su inocencia; y cuando todas estas cosas
me fueren contrarias, proferim'he al rey que darás una persona tuya
que haga armas con los tres malvados testigos; y no aprovechando
nada desto, probarás la fuerça en la que por ventura hallarás la
piedad que en el rey yo buscava. (p. 124)

The Cardinal attempts to reason with the King by combining social
and personal arguments and urging him to reconsider his decision
about Laureola: "porque mejor aciertan los honbres en las cosas agenas
que en las suyas propias, porque el coraçon de cuyo es el caso no puede
estar sin ira o cobdicia o afición o deseo o otras cosas semejantes, para
determinar como deve" (p. 130). The Cardinal continues by pointing
out the error:

Havemos sabido que quieres condenar a muerte a Laureola; si la
bondad no merece ser justiciada, en verdad tú eres injusto juez; no
quieras turbar tu gloriosa fama con tal juizio, que puesto que en él
huviese derecho, antes serías, si lo dieses, infamado por padre cruel
que alabado por rey justiciero...No seas verdugo de tu misma
sangre, que serás entre los honbres muy afeado. (p. 131)

The King, however, is adamant:

Bien sabéis que establecen nuestras leyes que la muger que fuere acusada de tal pecado muera por ello; pues ya veis cuánto más me conviene ser llamado rey justo que perdonador culpado (p. 133).

Laureola then writes to her father, claiming her innocence and willingness to die in order to prove it: "Si te place matarme por voluntad, óbralo, que por justicia no tienes por qué; la muerte que tú me dieres, aunque por causa de temor la rehúse, por razón de obedecer la consiento, haviendo por mejor morir en tu obediencia que bevir en tu desamor" (p. 138). She knows that she will be vindicated even if the vindication takes place after her death: "Tú serás llamado padre cruel y yo seré dicha hija innocente, que pues Dios es justo, él aclarará mi verdad; assí quedaré libre de culpa cuando haya recebido la pena" (p. 139).

This plea goes unheeded, so Leriano's only recourse is to proceed with his own sense of justice: to free Laureola by force and kill Persio, if necessary. When this is accomplished, Leriano, Laureola, and his knights are besieged at Susa by the King and his men. One of the liars confesses and the King is happy to pardon his daughter and Leriano. But, once again, he sends Leriano away so that he can pacify Persio's relatives. Yet again, the King permits his regard and misplaced loyalty (that is, concern for the family's honor) to interfere with any real sense of justice. Mirabella's father, in *Grisel y Mirabella*, tries again and again to execute justice, although his system of laws proves ineffective against the force of love. Here, it is not so much the laws that are at fault, or ineffective, as it is the King's willingness to interpret justice in his own way, one which is contradicted by the facts time and again. The King believed Persio rather than his daughter and Leriano; he interrupted the duel that Leriano was obviously winning; he ignored the significance of that duel, which is, as the Cardinal reminds him, that God had indicated the truth-teller. Even when Persio's accomplice confesses, the King still allows his feelings for Persio's family's honor to overshadow what should have been Leriano and Laureola's total vindication.

Leriano is consumed with passion and, along with the passion, the question of love's justice returns. Leriano dies of despair, as the rules of love would demand. His mother rages against this sense of justice and the work ends on an open note: Is this how love should treat a loyal servant? And, is it right that the natural order of things be reversed, that the young die before the old, even if it does happen in the name of love?

*Conclusion*

Each phase of desire in *Cárcel de Amor* brings with it an interpretation of justice. In the first phase, Leriano and Laureola struggle to decide who is right: should women protect their reputation at all costs or should they live up to the declared obligations of love, that they alleviate the victim's sufferings? This struggle is exemplified by the movement from country to court and back. In the second phase, God's justice and man's justice are compared. God's justice finally triumphs, as did Love's justice in the first part. This is illustrated by the example of the castle, or fortress, in each part. In the first part, when Laureola finally sends Leriano a letter, we are told that Leriano conquers his prison guards, one by one, and breaks out of the "Cárcel de Amor." The prison represents a tension between hope and despair, so Laureola's letter provides hope for the prisoner, thereby freeing him from Love's prison. Leriano reciprocates in the second part by conquering Persio, freeing Laureola, and holding out against the siege laid by her father. In this case, God's justice triumphs over the King's warped sense of justice, but to no avail.

In the third part, Leriano gives in to the unspoken demands of love, which even require death as the supreme form of fidelity and, in this case, protest against the injustice of the whole situation. The conflict in this part arises between the justice as Leriano sees it and as his mother sees it. A consideration of Rolfs' examination of suicide as a form of protest against cruel parents or cruel society is apt here: he claims that, in many works, a grieved community joins together after such a tragedy, or an oppressor is brought to justice.[27] If, in fact, Leriano's suicide makes an impression or brings the villain—the King—to justice, we certainly do not witness it. What we do see is an unresolved conflict about love and its treacherous, destructive nature.

---

[27] Daniel J. Rolfs, "Dante, Petrarch, Boccaccio and the Problem of Suicide," *RR*, 67 (1976), 200-25. As in the case of Ardanlier in *Estoria de dos amadores*, the moral question of suicide seems not to have been an issue. Whinnom tells us: "Aunque la Iglesia miraba el suicidio como un pecado mortal, no parece que el siglo XV lo tomase muy en serio. Diego de San Pedro mismo, al enumerar las mujeres virtuosas de la historia, incluye a varias suicidas, no sólo a las romanas sino también a doña María Coronel, española y cristiana," p. 38.

# 3

# Innovation Within Tradition:
# The Interplay of Love and Justice
# in Juan de Flores'
# *Grisel y Mirabella*

F THE SENTIMENTAL ROMANCES most frequently mentioned as monuments of the genre—*Siervo libre de amor, Arnalte y Lucenda, Cárcel de Amor, Grimalte y Gradissa*, and *Grisel y Mirabella*, the last one has sparked fewer analyses than the other four. This is hardly surprising since no less a critic than Menéndez y Pelayo dismissed *Grisel* with this curt evaluation: "Tal es la curiosa, aunque absurda, novela de Flores, cuyo éxito en el siglo XVI fue tan grande como es inexplicable hoy, considerando su flojo y desmalazado estilo."[1]

*Grisel y Mirabella* was, however, enormously popular. In 1925, Everett Ward Olmsted examined the European derivatives, tracing them back to the Italian version of the story: Lelio Aletiphilo's translation and modification of *Grisel, Historia de Isabella et Aurelio*, which served as a model for the anonymous English *Swetnam, the Woman-Hater*, the anonymous English *A Paire of Turtle Doves*, Scudéry's *Le Prince déguisé*, and Lope de Vega's *La ley ejecutada*.[2]

---

[1] Marcelino Menéndez y Pelayo, *Orígenes de la novela*, II (Madrid: CSIC, 1943), p. 63.

Barbara Matulka, in her monumental study of Flores' two works known at that time, *Grisel y Mirabella* and *Grimalte y Gradissa*, examined their widespread diffusion, proving beyond a doubt the overwhelming popularity of the former. Among her other major contributions are the catalogue of stock romance and folkloric motifs from which *Grisel y Mirabella* and *Grimalte y Gradissa* draw, and the comparisons she makes between Flores' use of these motifs and their use by other authors.[3] If one can find any fault with the study, it is that Matulka led later critics astray with her firm assertion that Flores was a profeminist author and that *Grisel* could be classified a profeminist work.[4] Thirty years later, a similar view is affirmed in Deyermond's history of medieval Spanish literature: Flores pronounces firmly in favor of the ladies, and the condemnation of Torrellas' cynicism is clear.[5]

In this chapter, the analysis of *Grisel y Mirabella* will show that the work is neither clearly profeminist nor antifeminist, but is fraught with ambiguities.[6] Flores establishes love relationships only to have them destroyed. Justice, the execution of social laws, seems to be an

[2] "Story of *Grisel and Mirabella*," in *Homenaje ofrecido a Menéndez Pidal: Miscelánea de estudios lingüísticos, literarios e históricos* (Madrid: Hernando, 1925), II, pp. 369-73.

[3] *The Novels of Juan de Flores and Their European Diffusion* (New York: Institute of French Studies, 1931). This study also contains an edition of *Grisel y Mirabella*. All quotations from *Grisel y Mirabella* are from Matulka's edition.

[4] Matulka expounds this notion further in "An Anti-Feminist Treatise of Fifteenth-Century Spain: Lucena's *Repetición de amores*," *RR*, 22 (1931), 96-116, in which she lists the pro and antifeminist writers of the century, placing Flores firmly with the profeminists.

[5] A. D. Deyermond, *A Literary History of Spain: The Middle Ages* (London: Ernest Benn, 1971), p. 166. It should be noted, however, that Deyermond does not claim that Flores is a feminist, merely that he feels the author sides with the ladies. To use the term feminist would be to confuse the issue when there really is an early feminist author, such as Teresa de Cartagena.

[6] Antony Van Beysterveldt's article "Revisión de los debates feministas del siglo XV y las novelas de Juan de Flores," *Hispania*, 64 (1981), 1-13, argues for a reconsideration of the sentimental romances as pro or antifeminist works because the view of women was invariable in these works. There is simply a difference between the degrees of compassion and charity with which women were treated in these works. He argues that *Grisel y Mirabella* is anti-courtly love because it is love which causes men to lose reason. The inferior reason of women was an accepted fact, so these works were not anti-women but anti-love. Although he refers to the "novels" of Juan de Flores in his title, he deals most specifically with the debate between Torrellas and Braçayda, and makes some general conclusions.

agent of destruction. Desire, a predominant theme of medieval narrative (and, obviously at the heart of sentimental romance), and the satisfaction of desire are juxtaposed to the meting out of justice. My analysis will focus first on *Grisel y Mirabella* as romance by discussing scenes of debate, community gatherings, and love relationships, and, second, the general theme as I see it: the struggle between desire and justice.[7]

*Grisel y Mirabella* shares with other sentimental romances some typical elements: the need for secrecy in love, the debate, cruel parent, exchange of letters, suicide, tragic ending, and the emphasis on love as the central issue. It should be noted, however, that the love relationship between Grisel and Mirabella is never the courtly, frustrated kind, but more like that of Liessa and Ardanlier in *Estoria de dos amadores*. A major part of *Grisel*, the debate between Braçayda and Torrellas, focuses on the vices (many) and the virtues (few) of women and men, an emphasis not found in the earlier *Siervo libre de amor*, but a prominent feature in Constable Pedro of Portugal's *Sátira de la felice e infelice vida*. Another major difference is the complete omission of first-person narrative. Even the setting is different: unlike the other romances' journey from court to country, *Grisel* takes place in the court and in the street, and in this sense is more akin to *La Celestina* than to the other sentimental romances.

In general, romance tends to move from a point of disorder to an expected one of harmonious resolution. Generally, romance is characterized by joyful recognition scenes, weddings, banquets, processions, or some other community celebration. The lovers are normally at the heart of the joyful celebration. *Grisel y Mirabella*, however, moves forward with a steady elimination of characters, the breakdown of all love relationships in the work, and an increasing chain of violence which ends with an inversion of the communal banquet. The women of the court accomplish their aim, but at what cost? It is a scene of grotesque mutilation and murder. It is also a scene of isolation, not harmony, since the men, except for the victim, are entirely excluded from it.

[7] I draw my examples of elements of romance and romance patterns from Northrop Frye's *The Secular Scripture: A Study of the Structure of Romance* (Cambridge, MA.: Harvard University Press, 1976; rpt. 1978).

*Debates and Community Scenes*

In *Grisel y Mirabella* there is a search for resolution through debate and the execution of harsh laws. Far from resolving the problem at hand, each debate ends either directly or indirectly in death. Grisel and Otro caballero challenge the veracity of each other's avowed love for Mirabella. The sad result of this rational exchange is the slaying of one friend by another. When Otro caballero suggests casting lots for Mirabella, the lofty nature of the dispute is deflated, becoming a parody of a combat of generosity. The combat of generosity is a typical motif of the romance of chivalry and some sentimental romances. Matulka connects the stock combat of generosity only with that of Grisel and Mirabella, in which each argues to be judged the guiltier of the two (p. 87). In declaring that Flores has transformed the typical story of two friends into two lovers, she neglects to mention the obvious parallel between the two male friends in *Grisel y Mirabella*. In the case of Grisel and Otro caballero, violence occurs instead of an act of generosity.

The true combat of generosity in the work, between the ill-fated lovers Grisel and Mirabella, serves two purposes. It confirms that they really do love each other: their generosity shows a noble side to their love which transcends passion. This does not, however, diminish the violence associated with their love. Their debate is a futile attempt to save each other. The result is merely a temporary delay of death.

From the particular debate of Grisel and Mirabella we move to the general debate between Torrellas and Braçayda on the vices of both sexes. The exchange is undertaken in order to determine a principle which can resolve a particular case. It is interesting that the debaters seem unconcerned by the recent show of loyalty by the young lovers. The accusations which each debater hurls at the other have nothing to do with the actual case at hand. Torrellas accuses women of seducing men, of employing coy techniques to lure men on, of being incapable of true reciprocity of affection. Braçayda accuses Torrellas in a similar fashion. The content of their debate consists of commonplaces of misogynist vituperation and specious reasoning by both parties. Torrellas' last barb is the trump card of misogynists, the linking of all women to Eve, for which women have no rejoinder. The judges decide that women are guilty of luring men to sins of carnality—therefore, Mirabella must pay the penalty.

Mirabella is a victim herself since it is a matter of record—the beginning of the story—that she did not overtly encourage anyone to pursue her. The beauty that kills was not of her choosing. Likewise, Grisel does not correspond to the portrait of man that Braçayda paints. Very little effort was necessary to encourage the love of Mirabella for Grisel.

Just as the debaters ignored the love Grisel and Mirabella show for each other, all involved seem unconcerned about the indisputable fact that several deaths occurred before Grisel and Mirabella became lovers, deaths associated with love, but not with seduction and wiles.

The outcome having been decided, Braçayda denounces the judges, pronouncing irreparable the schism between men and women. The Queen appeals to the King, who remains unmoved by her remarks. He is not portrayed as a cruel father of the type we see in *Estoria de dos amadores* but, originally, as one more victim of Mirabella's captivating beauty and, later, as a ruler who must, at all costs, enforce the laws of the land.

The Queen is enraged by this stolid show of acquiescence in the decision of the judges. She declares herself to be, from that point on, against the King, her husband. Thus, two more debates have ended in distressful irresolution. The debate between Torrellas and Braçayda ends with the decision that Mirabella must die. But that decision alienates the women from the men. There is no harmonious conclusion at this scene of a community gathering. In addition, this decision leads to the debate of the King and the Queen, which results in the individual alienation of husband and wife.

The next community scene is the procession to the stake. Parades and processions, in romance, are glittering spectacles producing, again, a feeling of community solidarity. Here, the glitter is present—Mirabella is bedecked in jewels and carried in a litter—but the mood is not at all joyful. The women, dressed in mourning, proceed together weeping, distinctly separated from the men. The irony of the procession is explicitly stated when the narrator tells us that the people expected to gather together like this for Mirabella's wedding, not her execution (p. 358).

Grisel and Mirabella address each other, speaking not the wedding vows one might expect in romance, but farewells before death. Before he can be restrained, Grisel leaps into the flames meant for his beloved. Mirabella's life can be spared by law since one of the two has paid with his life. The generosity of this pardon is meaningless to the heroine, who, alone in her room, explains, in a moving soliloquy, why she would not want to live without Grisel. Then, in the dark of night, while everyone sleeps, she jumps from the window to the courtyard.

The final public scene comes about when Torrellas hopes to initiate a relationship with Braçayda, and comes to the palace to visit her. This scene of dubious triumph for the ladies is a complete inversion of the romance banquet, which normally hails the newly-restored social order. The women are animal-like, resorting to a barbarism which, although achieving the goal of revenge, is a revolting act. Once again, a community scene in *Grisel y Mirabella* is not the harbinger of further harmony.

*Love in "Grisel y Mirabella": Violence and Death*

The dissolution of relationships is a primary, recurring event in the narrative of *Grisel*. Each relationship is somehow tainted by violence. The story begins with a "once upon a time" fairytale device, but soon after intrudes the first disturbing element. Mirabella's father does not allow his daughter to marry any one of the numerous suitors clamoring for her attention. Mirabella's beauty is such that all who see her fall in love with her. The King's knights are dying because of this love:

> y tan en stremo la amauan: que por su causa venian a perder las vidas. tanto que la flor de la caualleria de casa del Rey su padre fenecio sus dias en esta tal guerra. De manera que sopido por el Rey: la hizo meter en vn lugar muy secreto: que ningun baron ver la pudiesse: *por ser su vista muy peligrosa*. porque el desastre con buenas guardas se resiste. (p. 334)[8]

Beauty, love, and violence are associated from the outset of the work. The father's reluctance to marry his daughter even to a fine gentleman can, in part, be explained through the incest motif typical of romance.[9]

---

[8] The italics are mine. Martin S. Gilderman, in *Juan Rodríguez de la Cámara*, TWAS, 423 (Boston: Twayne, 1977), explains that Provençal poets considered women's beauty, which caused men to fall in love, to be good, or benevolent. In discussing Rodríguez del Padrón's *Siete gozos de amor* he notes: "Juan Rodríguez del Padrón interprets the spell of his lady's beauty as something powerful, attractive and yet malevolent; something which will lead him to his doom. This kind of female power, which is not present in either the Provençal or Castilian love lyrics, is present in neo-Celtic literature of the Middle Ages, in the ritual known as the *geiss*, in which young women of the upper nobility arbitrarily chose men of inferior or equal social status and imposed impossible tasks upon them which would ultimately lead to their death. The reward for the male's service could of course only be in the afterlife" (p. 33).

[9] In *The Secular Scripture* Frye explains that this is the complement to the

What is unique is the introduction of something negative or malevolent associated with the beauty of Mirabella herself. The King is simply one more prisoner of her beauty. He incarcerates her in the tower not because he does not want her to marry, since he could have done this much earlier if that were simply the case, but because she is causing the deaths of all his knights. The next relationship of which we become aware is the friendship between Grisel and Otro caballero. The two good friends quickly forget all feelings of camaraderie when faced with jealousy and desire for Mirabella. Grisel slays his friend, adding to the violence associated with Mirabella's beauty. Whether this is, in fact, a duel is ambiguous, as is the comment that "la flor de la caualleria... fenecio sus dias en esta tal guerra." The logical assumption is that all parties were engaged in duels over Mirabella, but Flores, who is not at all reticent about describing later deaths, is, I believe, deliberately silent about the actual cause of death, a silence which contributes to the ambiguity and mysteriousness associated with Mirabella's beauty. It is an example of the metaphor made real: instead of the verbal "dying of love" which pervades the *cancionero* love poetry, in *Grisel y Mirabella* and in other sentimental romances, people actually do die of love.[10]

The love between Grisel and Mirabella begins with a passionate encounter. The examination of sentiment, so prevalent in the romances of Diego de San Pedro, for example, and even Flores' other romance, *Grimalte y Gradissa*, does not occur here until much later, and even then, it is a public confession of sexual activity and not a lamentation of frustration and separation.

Mirabella cannot keep her exciting news to herself. She confides in her maid, who immediately reveals the secret to her own lover, the King's chief steward. The steward, we are told, is torn by his promise of secrecy to the maid and his dismay at the dishonor done to his master, the King. However, what propels him to action is envy. The maid's loyalty to Mirabella is subverted by passion; that of the chief steward to his beloved by envy. The envy is not explained, but it may well be that Mirabella's beauty has claimed another victim:

Oedipal complex, and need not involve sexual activity, but a sense of possessiveness on the part of the father or the daughter. See, for example, pp. 104-05, and 137.

[10] Theodore L. Kassier studied this literary device in, *"Cancionero* Poetry and *La Celestina*: From Metaphor to Reality," *Hispanófila*, 56 (1976), 1-28. The "dying of love" metaphor is made explicit in Nicolás Núñez's continuation of *Cárcel de Amor*, contained in *Dos opúsculos isabelinos*, ed. Keith Whinnom, Exeter Hispanic Texts, 22 (Exeter University, 1979), pp. 51-92.

esta camarera suya amaua mucho ahun maestrasala del Rey y como
supo el secreto de su senyora: no pudo su lealdad tanto soffrir: que
no lo descobriesse al su amante lo que Mirabella y Grisel passauan. y
ell vyendo tan grande error: doliendo se mucho dela honra de su
senyor: o poruentura de inuidia mouido: no pudo callar lo que al Rey
no publicasse la maldad que en su casa Grisel cometia. el qual como
oyo tan feo caso: con grande discrecion busco manera como amos los
tomassen en vno. (p. 337)

Grisel and Mirabella, captured by the King's guards, are to be tried
for having transgressed a law of the land. No matter how we feel about
the protagonists and the rightness or wrongness of their love, it is true
that their act of passion has led them to an ultimate violence—the
death of one of them.

The King becomes alienated from his wife and daughter by his
adherence to strict justice. The alienation is merely one more link in
the chain of disintegrating relationships which can be traced back to
the succumbing of Grisel and Mirabella to an overwhelming passion
initiated by Mirabella's beauty: "por ser su vista muy peligrosa."

Torrellas and Braçayda move from utter hatred to a love of sorts. It
has already been explained that Braçayda never cares for Torrellas,
although he seems to have become enamored of her, even if it is simply
lust. It is a stroke of luck for the Queen that Torrellas claims to love
Braçayda. The Queen sets in motion the plan that will avenge her
daughter's death.

At this point we see the savagery which can be associated with
motherlove. Mirabella's mother loses all sense of reason, all dignity, by
resorting to the kind of carnage expected only of animals.[11] The
passion inspired by Mirabella's beauty leads to a dissolution of family
ties, the bonds of friendship, love between husband and wife, the
loyalty of lover to lover and servant to mistress, and, in an ugly finale, a
transformation of the expected gentleness and purity of motherlove.

### Death and Narrative Space in "Grisel y Mirabella"

The violent events in the story are described in increasing detail as
the narrative progresses. There are five deaths in the work, if we count
as one event the remark of the narrator that the King's knights are
dying "en esta tal guerra."

---

[11] Or, as Deyermond has suggested, there may be a relationship to the wild
man/wild woman of art and folklore. See "El hombre salvaje en la novela
sentimental," *Filología*, 10 (1964), 97-111.

The next death is only slightly more specific in description. The knights are unnamed, although it is soon learned, after the fact, that one is Grisel. The description is, however, more than the remark that the knights are dying. Here, one friend slays another:

Estos dos caualleros de pues de hauer mucho questionado quien mas dignamente la [Mirabella] merecia: vinieron en tan grandes rompimientos de palabras: que el que no consentio en las suertes: mato al otro. y tan secreta fue la question entre ellos. que iamas el Rey pudo saber quien lo hauia muerto. Aquell cauallero vencedor llamauan Grisel. (p. 337)

In the case of the next death, Grisel's suicide is described, although not in great detail:

Como Grisel dio fin asus palabras: procuro de dar fin asu vida. y en el fuego de biuas llamas se lanço sin ningun temor. tanto que ahun que remediar lo quiziessen non fue cosa possible. y Mirabella lo quizo seguir. mas Braçayda. y las otras damas y donzellas que con ella stauan: delas llamas del fuego afuerça la quitaron. y luego la Reyna con otros caualleros llegaron a supplicar al Rey perdonar la quiziesse. y pues que del cielo vino por marauilloso milagro dar muerte a quien la merecia: que contra la voluntad de Dios no diesse pena a quien no la mereçe. Alo qual el Rey no atorgaua ni contradezia. saluo lo remetio alos de su conseio. con los quales ligero fue de alcançar no diessen la muerte a Mirabella. si ella despues no la buscara. La qual como vio sacar del fuego asu amado Grisel: no se como scriua las llastimas que ella dixo. (pp. 361-62)

Mirabella laments her lover's death, venting her anguish in a soliloquy similar to the one uttered by Rojas' Melibea. The description is enlarged: we are told her plan, her motivation, her clothing, the timing, and the manner. Not wanting to live without Grisel, Mirabella waits until, at night, the court is asleep:

Y vna noche la postremera de sus dias non podiendo el amor y muerte de Grisel soffrir: por dar fin a sus congoxas: la dio a su vida. la qual spero tiempo que los que la guardauan dormiessen. y como ella vyo el tiempo dispuesto y en su libertad fuesse en camisa a vna ventana que miraua sobre vn corral donde el Rey tenia vnos leones y entre ellos se dexo caher. los quales non vsaron con ella de aquella obediencia: que ala sangre real deuian. segun en tal caso los suelen loar, mas antes miraron a su fambre: que ala realeza de Mirabella. a quien ninguna mesura cataron. y muy presto fue dellos spedaçada. y delas delicadas carnes cada uno contento el apetito. Y despues que

recordaron los que a Mirabella guardauan y vieron que en la cama
no staua: temieron aquello que depues fallaron verdad. Y como la
Reyna y las damas vieron la beldad de aquella donzella crudamente
feneçer de tan rauiosa muerte: sin scriuir esta bueno de presumir el
stremo y grandeza de sus llantos. pero porque yo non podria tan
dolorosas cosas como eran figurar: non quiero sino dexar lo a quien
pensar lo podiere (p. 363)

Once again, there is ambiguity here, of the kind found in the description of the knights' deaths and Mirabella's glance or the sight of her.
Lions, Kings of all beasts, possess the quality of being able to recognize
royalty. Here, they ignore that and devour her. Is their lack of
recognition an oversight or is it indicative, perhaps, of some culpability
on Mirabella's part or of the malevolence associated with her beauty?
The lions devour her—an image which is also connected with sexual
activity. The author is, perhaps, establishing a connection between the
King, Mirabella's father, whose own lustful, jealous feelings may be
coming into play in his refusal to spare his daughter and the King of
the beasts who eats her up.

The fifth and final death scene takes up the most narrative space:

Estando Braçayda en tal razonamiento: vino la Reyna con todas sus
damas que en asechança estauan de Torrellas. Y aquell despues de
arrebatado hataron lo de pies y de manos: que ninguna defiença de
valer se touo. y fue luego despoiado de sus vestidos y ataparon le la
boca porque quexar non se pudiesse. y desnudo fue ahun pilar bien
atado. y alli cada una trahia nueua inuencion para le dar tormentos.
y tales houo que con tenazas ardiendo: y otras con vnyas y dientes
rauiosamente le despedeçaron. estando assi medio muerte por creçer
mas pena en su pena non le quisieron de vna vez matar porque las
crudas y fieras llagas se le refriassen: y otras de nueuo viniessen y
depues que fueron ansi cansadas de tormentar le: de grande reposo
la Reyna y sus damas a çenar se fueron alli çerca dell. . . y trayendo
ala memoria sus maliciosas obras: cada una dezia ala Reyna que no
les parecia que quantas muertes ad aquell mal hombre se pudiessen
dar porque passasse largos anyos: non cumpliria ahun que cada
noche de aquellas penitencias ouiesse. y otras dezian mil maneras de
tormentos cada qual como le agradaua. y tales cosas passauan entre
ellas que por cierto yo stimo que ellas dauan al cuytado de Torrellas
mayor pena que la muerte misma. y ansi vino a soffrir tanta pena
delas palabras: como delas obras. y despues que fueron alçadas todas
las mesas fueron iuntas a dar amarga cena a Torrellas. Y tanto fue
todas seruido con potages y aues y maestre sala: que non se como
scriuir las differencias delas iniurias y offienças que le hazian. y esto

duro hasta quel dia esclarecio. y despues que no dexaron ninguna carne en los huessos: fueron quemados. y de su seniza guardando cada qual vna buxeta por reliquias de su enemigo. y algunas houo que por cultre en el cuello la trahian. porque trayendo mas a memoria su vengança mayor plazer houiessen. Ansi que la grande malicia de Torrellas dio alas damas victoria. y a ell pago de su merecido. (pp. 369-70)

It has been suggested that this scene has an ironic parallel in the Last Supper.[12] In keeping with the rest of *Grisel y Mirabella*, there is an inversion of the romance ritual celebration. The banquet is grotesque: the women work up an appetite by torturing and clawing Torrellas apart. There are overtones of cannibalism; the women did not devour him, but they did set out their dinner in full view of the human being they were in the process of mutilating with their nails and teeth. The imagery suggests demonic qualities. First of all, fire is associated with women and the devil. Alfonso Martínez de Toledo's *Corbacho* is full of sensual imagery linked to diabolic images of infernal fire, which in turn is linked to imagery about women.[13] In addition, women, on account of their heritage of Eve, are associated both with food and with the devil. In this scene, there is a plethora of images which convey an evil, repulsive picture of women. They claw Torrellas like animals; when they tire of this, they immediately think of food. Women's love of food is not only found in *Corbacho*. Bernat Metge (c. 1346-1413), quoted by Matulka (p. 31), stated that women were gluttonous and ordered long, refined menus of delicate dishes. In *Grisel y Mirabella*, the women are merely living up to their unsavory reputation.[14]

[12] Deyermond, *History*, p. 166.

[13] See Colbert I. Nepaulsingh, "Talavera's Imagery and the Structure of the *Corbacho*," *RCEH*, 4, no. 3 (1980), 329-49 in which he notes the frequent association between diabolic imagery and women.

[14] One ambiguous statement is possibly another example of the metaphor made real. The word "maestresala" means chief waiter according to contemporary usage. In Joan Corominas' *Diccionario crítico etimológico de la lengua castellana*, III (Madrid: Gredos, 1956), p. 186a, we find, under the heading *maestro*, this example: "gastronómico (maestresala)." In *Grisel y Mirabella* it also appears as "maestrasala" and is used in two ways. The person who initially betrays Grisel and Mirabella is identified as "maestrasala." He is not seen again, and, when we get to the scene of the cannibalistic banquet-murder of Torrellas, we are told that the women set out a meal of "potages, aues, y maestresala." I hesitate to suggest that the main fare along with the soup and chickens was the chief steward, but there does not appear to be another translation of the word.

The only sense of time related here is when the women taunt Torrellas with recollections of his past deeds and "esto duro hasta quel dia esclarecio." In practical terms, the women would have to pick a time when they would not be thwarted. Nighttime, however, is the time of the devil and the women continued until dawn when "no dexaron ninguna carne en los huessos." The importance of the contrast between day and night would probably not escape the notice of the reader familiar with Christian imagery. As St. Paul reminds us: "The night is far spent, the day is at hand: let us therefore cast off the works of darkness, and let us put on the armour of light" (Romans 13:12).

By the mention of the remains of Torrellas as a relic, this final scene takes on the additional ironic parallel of a saint's martyrdom. It is the ultimate inversion contributing to *Grisel's* ambiguity.

The last line seems to be the narrator's agreement that justice was done: "Ansi que la grande malicia de Torrellas dio alas damas victoria: y a ell pago de su merecido." It is possible that, in view of the imagery at the end, there is either an ironic or an ambivalent viewpoint. Flores may well have sympathized with the women but if so, then he fell into the trap of portraying them as their accusers would have done. There is another possibility. At the end of *Corbacho*, Martínez de Toledo recants his accusations of the earlier parts of the work.[15] He says that some women attacked him and prevailed upon him to retract his statements. In doing so he may have been truthful or, as E. Michael Gerli maintains, it may have been one more example of the women's evil ability to terrorize.[16] What the author is doing, in Gerli's view, is

---

[15] There is controversy about the authenticity of the epilogue to Martínez de Toledo's *Corbacho*. The major objections and affirmations are set forth in E. Michael Gerli's *Alfonso Martínez de Toledo*, TWAS, 398 (Boston: Twayne, 1976), pp. 31-35. I agree with Gerli's view that "the matter is very subtle indeed, and that the first impression usually evoked by the passage [the Archipriest's palinode] may contain implications not yet fathomed by its critics.... As Miss [Christine] Whitbourn herself points out, stylistically the epilogue shares many common characteristics with the rest of the *Whip* [Corbacho]... When examined in the light of contemporary amatory literature, the epilogue contains nothing truly at odds with Martínez' intended lesson" (pp. 33-34).

[16] Gerli asserts: "In the epilogue to the *Archpriest of Talavera*, the gentle ladies conquer and force the narrator to admit his error, but not without first having to resort to verbal abuse, terror, and physical violence to extract his confession—the very things they are insistently rebuked for in the body of the work.... With a malicious twinkle in his eye, he could well have sacrificed himself to the enemy in order to show the error of their ways" (pp. 34-35).

emphasizing by dint of alleged actual experience the truth of that which he wrote earlier in his work regarding the nature of women. Flores may be paying lip service to the ostensible victory of the women while having successfully painted them as animal-like creatures.

Torrellas' death is presented as the culmination of the deaths previously described, whose elements appear in some form in this final scene. At least one aspect of each of the other deaths can be found in the spectacular torture-murder of Torrellas. The knights died somehow because of an entrapment by Mirabella's beauty. Otro caballero, like Torrellas, was slain during the night by a friend. His words were the cause of his death, since Grisel found offensive the suggestions made by Otro caballero. Because of Torrellas' verbal debasement of women, resulting, ultimately, in Mirabella's suicide, the Queen sought his death. Grisel's suicide was a leap into the flames (like the flames of love), while Torrellas was tortured by "fieras llagas." After Mirabella's leap during the night into the courtyard, hungry lions devoured every inch of her flesh, leaving only her bones. Her mother and ladies-in-waiting, metamorphosed by rage into lion-like creatures, clawed the flesh from Torrellas' bones until none remained.

The increase in detail of the five deaths is the result of a carefully-planned narrative technique. Pamela Waley attributes the lack of specific detail in the other deaths to Flores' reserve about portraying gore.[17] This is not the case at all. The tale of Grisel and Mirabella is one of increasing violence, of increasing chaos, which subverts the legal controls which the characters attempt to impose on it. The momentum gained by violence initiated by Mirabella's beauty grows, and is reflected by the increasing amount of narrative space dedicated to it, until the tale ends with the grotesque mutilation of an unpleasant character.

### "Grisel y Mirabella" as System: The Interplay of Love and Justice

The issue of pro and antifeminist conventions of the fifteenth century seems to be a diversion from the essence of Flores' work: here, there is no unqualified support of either men or women. In fact, the

---

[17] She states, in her edition of Flores' Grimalte y Gradissa (London: Tamesis, 1971): "The torments of Fiometa [in Grimalte y Gradissa], the tortures inflicted on Grisel and Mirabella, and the murder of Torrellas are described in horrific but very general terms, and Flores sometimes prefers reticence, 'porque yo no podria tan dolorosas cosas como eran figurar, non quiero sino dexarlo a quien pensarlo podiere" (p. xliv).

clichés of the debate between Torrellas and Braçayda—well-known to
any reader of the time, to judge by their frequency—serve to deflect
reader attention from the subtle nature of what is actually at the heart
of the matter. *Grisel y Mirabella* is about extremes: about desire, about
passion, and the futile attempts to control its resultant chain of
violence. Flores' work is a demythification of love: its problematic
nature is examined, as is that of the King's answer to the discord
produced by love. It is about the battle between the emotions, the non-
rational, and the reliance man has on justice, the rational, to determine
the guilty party in order to right whatever goes wrong.

*Grisel y Mirabella* is about two extreme measures which lead to the
same end: love and justice as expressed by the King and love and justice
as expressed by the Queen. It is the same end, incidentally, which came
from desire, the initial impulse of the story. In fact, it becomes
increasingly difficult to distinguish between the concepts of love and
justice and the actions they provoke. For example, when the King
incarcerates Mirabella, is it simply for society's protection or is there a
selfish reason? When the Queen kills Torrellas, is it from love of her
daughter or from a higher sense that justice must be done? Is there any
real difference, since they all lead to violent deaths?

Desire inspires a chaotic momentum of violence which whirls out of
the characters' control—if it is a force which can ever be subject to
control. The men, symbolized by the just King, assume that desire can
be controlled by the execution of laws. When the "Ley de Escocia" fails
to pinpoint the guiltier lover, the King continues in the same vein by
calling for a debate on the guilt of men or women in general.

When Torrellas and Braçayda arrive in Scotland, the opposing
parties plead their cases somewhat early. The Queen openly attempts
to influence Braçayda in favor of her daughter: the women of the court
entertain Braçayda at great feasts. The King maintains the decorum of
a King by not partaking in the attempts to bribe Torrellas, but he does
not stop them. The narrator hints at ignoble motives in that these men
were impelled by their hatred of Mirabella to seek her conviction:

> Principalmente algunos caualleros de aquella tierra a quien continuo
> crecia enemiga con Mirabella. porque su grande beldad hauia sido
> causa: como muchos se hauian perdido en la requesta y seguimiento
> famoso de aquella amorosa batalla. por esto rogauan a Torrellas: que
> defendiesse su partido. lo qual supo bien contentar: y satisfazer alos
> apetitos de cadauno dellos. y ansi andauan la Reyna y sus damas con
> Braçayda. y los caualleros con Torrellas fauoreciendo cadauno su
> partido. (p. 343)

A major theme of *Grisel* crystallizes in two scenes: that of the judges entering the room to make their pronouncement and that of the murder of Torrellas. The latter has already been described in detail. The other scene presents a powerful image:

> Grandes altercaciones passaron entre Torrellas y Braçayda: mas delas que ninguno podria scriuir. y vistas por los iuezes las razones de amas partes: tomaron determinacion para dar la sentencia, los quales ya despues de complidos: vinieron cubiertos de luto. y vnas spadas manzilladas de sangre. en sus diestras manos. con otras muchas serimonias. segund en aquella tierra se acostumbra. Y eran dotze iuezes: los quales dieron sentencia: que Mirabella muriesse. y fundaron por muchas razones ser ella en mayor culpa que Grisel. Y como en presencia dela Reyna delante sus damas fuesse condemnada a muerte: las vozes que scomençaron a dar: ponian tal tristeza en los animos: que parecia el sol scurecer se. y el cielo querer dello tomar sentimiento. (p. 355)

The two scenes represent an overall view of justice in the text: the repressed violence, in the name of reason and justice, of the judges with their blood-stained swords, and the women at the end of *Grisel*, in the name of vengeance, committing acts of unmitigated barbarity.

Here are two extreme actions: the King organizing a debate in which the odds are clearly in the men's favor, and the Queen coldly planning and executing her horrific night of revenge. Flores juxtaposes a primitive sacrificial rite—Torrellas' murder—and the more modern, acceptable ritual—the debate and execution—which masks the collective need for a sacrificial victim. The transgression of a law should not, of necessity, call for the death of the offender. But there is a social need, as evidenced here, for a punishment which also acts as the release for the collective subconscious cry for blood.[18] The women need no pretense of law and order for their bloodthirstiness—like the lions, they know exactly what they are after, and they find it.

But the role of justice fares not much better here. As René Girard says: "Centuries can pass before men realize that there is no real difference between their principle of justice and the concept of re-

---

[18] René Girard's *Violence and the Sacred*, trans. Patrick Gregory (Baltimore: Johns Hopkins University Press, 1977; rpt. 1979), is an anthropological-literary study of religion and violence. Although the work as a whole treats the rise of religion and justice, justice is most cogently discussed in the chapter entitled "Sacrifice," pp. 1-38.

venge" (p. 24). The men believe that they are comporting themselves according to the laws of the land, but we have seen already that similar images are evoked in the scene of Mirabella's death and the lobbying of Torrellas that the men performed. Torrellas assures the men that he "supo contentar: y satisfazer alos apetitos de cadauno dellos" (p. 343). Later, as we know, when the lions ate Mirabella, "delas delicadas carnes cada uno contento el apetito" (p. 363). The behavior of the women at the end of the text evokes images of the lions as well, but, if the women were overtly animal-like in their act of revenge, the men are only more subtly so. Neither men, as the voices of reason, nor women, who initially attempt reason and turn to something else, are victorious here.

Flores indicates that women are more to blame than men, not because the judges say so, but because he shows Mirabella's beauty to be malevolent from the start, inspiring a violent passion. But Mirabella, too, is a victim of her own beauty. The real blame falls on the lovers who succumb to their passionate impulses, thereby setting in motion a violent chain of events, which might have been curtailed by the King's incarceration of Mirabella, removing her from the sight of men. If there is ambiguity in this, it is because there exists no simple answer. If passion is uncontrollable, can we blame Mirabella for her beauty or Grisel for searching for her? Does the blame begin when they fall prey to their sexuality and begin an affair?

Women lose doubly in this text. Not only does desire, a destructive force, begin with women, but women are shown to resort to savagery. Even if men mask savagery behind a public debate (an act no less morally reprehensible than that of the women), it would appear nonetheless that the mask of civilization is preferable to the inevitable comparisons with the hungry lions that the women suffer.

But men in this text have their faults, as we have seen. The King initially refuses to give his daughter in marriage. Torrellas feigns love for Braçayda in order to satisfy lust. Also, as stated earlier, the debate evidences a repressed violence, since the rational judges appear with bloodstained swords.

The confusion in *Grisel y Mirabella* and the interpretations critics have proposed are a consequence of the characters' and the readers' joint assumption that there is clearly a wrong and a right: either men are guilty or women are guilty. The women characters assume, even after the disastrous end of both protagonists, that there exists some kind of solace in another violent act and that there can be justification for one. They assume that there is one culpable person—Torrellas— who is morally responsible for what has occurred, although clearly he can take no responsibility for the deaths caused by Mirabella's beauty and by Grisel's anger towards his friend.

What is incontrovertible, however, is that critics as well as characters have been fooled. Matulka, joining forces with the women in the work, sees them as triumphant, although enough clues are provided to the ambiguities and complexities of the work to show that there is no clearcut answer. In an article on *A Midsummer Night's Dream* Girard explains that the lovers are not blameless, although they themselves see only the external obstacles, and that the midsummer night is one of increasing violence due to the destructive nature of desire. As to the role of the reader in this, Girard explains it well:

> As long as the standard plot is vaguely outlined, even in the crudest and least believable fashion, the author can subvert his own myths and state the truth at every turn, with no consequences whatsoever. The audience will instinctively and automatically rally around the old clichés, so completely blind and deaf to everything which may contradict them that the presence of this truth will not even be noticed. The continued misunderstanding of the play throughout the centuries gives added resonance to the point Shakespeare is secretly making, providing ironic confirmation that the most worn-out myth will always triumph over the most explicit demythification.[19]

In *Grisel y Mirabella* we have a perfect analogy: blameless young lovers are thwarted by a cruel father and a cruel fate, only to be avenged by a Queen and her court. This interpretation is as much a fairytale as the tale itself. The obstacles are not the cruel father, or the misogynist Torrellas, or even fate. Grisel and Mirabella's problems begin at the same point desire does. But Matulka's conclusion is not surprising, since it is a straightforward interpretation of the chronological events of the work, and since it satisifes the reader's need for closure, the need to see that the text has come to some satisfactory end.

In her study on nonsense literature, in which she examined some literary principles which are applicable to other kinds of literature as well, Susan Stewart shows how one principle, infinite causality, is terminated only by the ad hoc addition of an ending. In children's literature, the rhymes and poems of infinite chains, the ending is

---

[19] "Myth and Ritual in Shakespeare: *A Midsummer Night's Dream*," in *Textual Strategies: Perspectives in Post-Structuralist Criticism*, ed. Josué V. Harari (Ithaca: Cornell University Press, 1979; rpt. 1984), pp. 189-212, at pp. 194-95.

arbitrary.[20] If we see *Grisel Y Mirabella* as a tale of vengeance triumphant, then we can be satisifed with the turn of events, viewing them
as a morally satisfying conclusion to the chain of occurrences. If,
however, we see something more, as I think we must, not permitting
ourselves to be fooled by Flores' abrupt ending, then we will be left
with the feeling that the chain of violence has not ended with Torrellas'
death, that perhaps, with the onslaught of primitive savagery, social
harmony is still a long way off.

*Conclusion*

To sum up, Flores refuses to provide easy answers, but we can
come to some conclusions, once we admit the ambiguities which exist
in the work. The ambiguities are the consequence of the tensions
established in *Grisel y Mirabella*. Flores sets up a system which he
undermines along the way. The primary system is that of the material
of romance, read as Matulka reads it. It consists of a series of elements
easily associated with well-known literature, such as the romances of
chivalry. This system is consistently undercut by subtle (and not-so-
subtle) qualifications and ambiguities associated with the characters,
their actions, and the imagery that surrounds them. The second
manner of undercutting, which can perhaps be called the true system
of *Grisel y Mirabella*, is in the process of the conflation of love and justice
and their inextricable link to violence.

*Grisel y Mirabella* demythifies love: it is not a simple tale of two
young lovers thwarted by external forces. Love, better named desire,
brings with it unexpectedly bitter results, which are never seen in, for
example, the romances of chivalry, and are not fully explored in the
*cancionero* love poetry which glorifies violence--the poetry of "muero
porque no muero." Here, the paradox is brought to life and shows its
violent nature. In *Grisel y Mirabella*, women cause desire and, once
begun, desire runs its own course—the course of disaster.

If there is another process of demythification in the text, it is one
that implies that the solution often rivals the problem in its destruc-
tiveness. Justice is not the solution to every social ill, since, in this case,

[20] *Nonsense: Aspects of Intertextuality in Folklore and Literature* (Baltimore: Johns
Hopkins University Press, 1979). In "Desire and Causality in Medieval Narrative," *RR*, 71 (1980), 213-43, Evelyn Birge Vitz shows how medieval texts are
resolved according to the satisfaction of a character, or characters, and to the
satisfaction of the reader.

it contributes to the disasters already begun by desire alone. Reason is often as violent as the overt violence shown by the women of the court.

Every action or rationale is pushed to an ultimate point. The lions are emblematic of the kind of extreme found in the work. In attacking Mirabella, "ninguna mesura cataron;" ignoring completely her royal status, they gobbled her up. Those three words—"ninguna mesura cataron"—suit some aspect of every character. Nothing, with the possible exception of the King's incarceration of Mirabella in the tower, befits the noble quality of *mesura*, and even this action is qualified by the shadow of the incest motif. The incarceration is the only half-measure taken, but desire is too strong for it to control, proving utterly without foundation the narrator's remark, "porque el desastre con buenas guardas se resiste." After that, all actions and responses are extremes. Even the debate, the attempt to invoke reason, is an extreme—death is the only possible penalty for one of the lovers. The general conclusion is that extreme measures, no matter what their other name—desire, justice, barbarity—result in mankind's destruction.

# 4

# The Real and the Written:
# Mimetic Desire in Juan de Flores'
## *Grimalte y Gradissa*

E HAVE SEEN in the studies of San Pedro's *Arnalte y Lucenda* and *Cárcel de Amor* that mimetic desire—the action of imitating an ideal or rival—functions as a primary impulse in the actions of the male characters.[1] The female characters—Lucenda in *Arnalte y Lucenda* and Laureola in *Cárcel de Amor*—tend to react to the approaches of the male protagonists rather than initiate the love interest themselves.[2] This is not to say that imitation plays no part in the women's actions. When they do respond to their pursuers, either verbally or by letter, they may indeed be following a prescribed format or model of behavior.[3]

---

[1] The notions of imitated and spontaneous desire, according to René Girard's definitions, are explained in Chapter II of this study.

[2] I refer specifically to the women who are objects of desire in the two texts, not to all female characters in the text. The mothers of Leriano and Laureola (*Cárcel de Amor*) take steps to investigate the charges against their children, but this role is very different from that of the women involved in love triangles. Belisa's unusual role in *Arnalte y Lucenda* has been discussed in Chapter II.

[3] San Pedro's *Arnalte y Lucenda* and both Flores' romances were dedicated to the ladies as examples of behavior. This dedication presumes a reality: were the ladies of the court conducting affairs of love service so that they would need these texts as exemplary stories?

What is of primary concern here, however, is that process of desire, be it spontaneous or imitated, which leads to disaster. As we have seen in the works already examined, when desire leads to a physical relationship, the result is what I have termed violent love. Desire which is not fulfilled physically leads to frustration and never to a new or renewed love interest.[4]

*Grimalte y Gradissa*, Juan de Flores' ambitious, highly unusual and artistically-successful work, embodies the conflict of mimetic desire. But the popularity of the work with the audience in the final decade of the fifteenth century appears to have been minimal. Only one edition of *Grimalte y Gradissa* survives, although, in addition to this, Barbara Matulka mentions Maurice Scève's translation of *Grimalte* and its possible influence on *Délie*, and Pamela Waley illustrates convincingly the influx of material from *Grimalte* to the early sixteenth-century editions of *Tristán de Leonís*.[5]

Flores transforms the narrative technique so apparent in *Grisel y Mirabella*—the juxtaposition of pairs of lovers and the use of multiple debates and deaths—into one in which the characters themselves are aware of its literary nature. Within *Grimalte y Gradissa*, the primary

---

[4] The implications of this dichotomy have been examined indirectly in each of the analyses presented thus far. My conclusions about this phenomenon will be discussed in the final chapter of this study in the hope of providing a new framework within which to view the troublesome genre known as sentimental romance.

[5] Matulka, *The Novels of Juan de Flores* and Waley, "Juan de Flores y *Tristán de Leonís*," *Hispanófila*, no. 12, (May 1961), 1-14, in which she suggests that the printed texts of *Tristan* may descend from a reworking by Flores. A more recent discovery made by Harvey L. Sharrer, "Letters in the Hispanic Prose *Tristan* Texts: Iseut's Complaint and Tristan's Reply," *Tristania*, 7 (1981-82), 3-20, gives strong evidence that Flores may indeed have been an active participant in the development of Arthurian material in Spain. Contained in a MS collection along with, among other works, a copy of Flores' *Triumpho de Amor* (see my article, "Juan de Flores' Other Work: Technique and Genre of *Triumpho de Amor*," *JHP*, 5 [1980-81], 25-40) were two fragments of letters; *Carta enviada por Hiseo la Brunda a Tristan de Leonis quexandose del porque la dexo presa a su causa y se caso con Hiseo de las Blancas Manos* and *Respuesta de Tristan desculpandose de la innocente culpa que le encargan*. Professor Sharrer's hypothesis that these letters are, in fact, the work of Juan de Flores himself seems to me to be highly provocative and important for scholars of both the sentimental romances and Arthurian literature in Spain. In Chapter I, I mentioned the link between Arthurian material and the sentimental romance in connection with Juan Rodríguez del Padrón's probable debt to the Tristan legend.

juxtaposition is that of two autobiographies. *L'Elegia di Madonna Fiam-metta*, the fourteenth-century work by Boccaccio, is the feigned auto-biography of the female protagonist. Gradissa reads *Fiammetta* and is influenced by this sad tale, so much so that she charges her own lover, Grimalte, to help to bring Pamphilo and Fiometa back together. Flores claims that *Grimalte* itself is an autobiography, asserting in the opening line of the prologue that he has changed his name to Grimalte for this work. The change seems capricious at first, but it quickly becomes apparent that it is not. The name-change creates the sense of two entities, author as distinct from character, while remind-ing the reader that they are one and the same. Pamela Waley suggests that it is done in imitation of Boccaccio's façade:

> Flores refers to *Fiammetta*, not by name, but as "famosa scriptura." Having ignored the creator behind the creation, Flores in turn conceals himself behind a character of his own story and calls himself, "por la siguiente obra," Grimalte. This preservation of the illusion of reality conforms with Boccaccio's consciously adopted narrative of pseudo-autobiography.[6]

The view expressed by Barbara Weissberger seems nearer the mark:

> What is unconventional in this introduction is the way Flores exposes, with artful candor, the illusion of reality necessary to the autobiographical form of his romance. By pointing out to the reader that the name Grimalte is merely a pseudonym, Flores makes explicit what in previous romances of the sentimental genre was implicit: that very process of fictionalization whereby the "yo" of the real author becomes the "yo" of a character. We have here an initial tear in the work's fabric of illusion, a tear that will gradually widen as the narrative unfolds.[7]

Whereas in *Grisel y Mirabella* Flores sets up a system—a straight-forward story—and undercuts it by way of imagery and ambiguous scenes and statements as he goes along, a different process of under-

[6] "Juan de Flores and the Evolution of Spanish Fiction in the Fifteenth Century," unpublished dissertation, Westfield College, University of London, 1968, p. 173. For further discussion of Flores' debt to Boccaccio, see her article, "Fiammetta and Panfilo Continued," *IS*, 24 (1969), 15-31, and Chapter 2 of the introduction to her edition of *Grimalte y Gradissa* (London: Tamesis, 1971), "The Influence of Boccaccio in *Grimalte y Gradissa*," pp. xxviii-xlv.

[7] "Authors, Characters and Readers in *Grimalte y Gradissa*," in *Creation and Re-creation: Experiments in Literary Form in Early Modern Spain*, ed. Ronald E. Surtz and Nora Weinerth (Newark, Delaware: Juan de la Cuesta, 1983), pp. 61-76, at pp. 67-68.

cutting reveals itself in *Grimalte y Gradissa*. Flores confuses reality, making it impossible to sort out the literary from the real within the text. The problem is compounded by the fact that, for the characters themselves, there exist at least two literary realities, an ideal "real" and a real "real." The ideal "real" consists of a courtly code—a code of love service—embodied in the *cancionero*-type love poetry which stemmed from a social reality. Roger Boase tells us that the poets of *cancionero* love verse believed their work to express a truth, a historical reality.[8] Just as courtly love, with various rules and modifications depending on the epoch, the country and, presumably, the individuals, was a social and historical phenomenon, so, too, poetry was the means of expressing the emotions underlying this truthful phenomenon. In Gradissa's case, the real "real" is, of course, Fiammetta/Fiometa's autobiography which, because of the power of the written word, impels Gradissa to abandon the contrived—as we see it—or the ideal "real" of poetry for another kind of reality, an observable one, a provable one. There occurs a transformation of her view that love in the courtly sense is an ideal perspective of love. Fiometa and Pamphilo, by virtue of their adulterous, sensual relationship, cannot be seen as models of conduct in the courtly sense. Gradissa abandons her role as the courtly lady for a role as behind-the-scenes manipulator of events in order to provide aid for the adulterous Fiometa in her passionate quest. Gradissa is thus admitting another perspective on love, one which leads to something more than the worship from afar. Love service, in the sense of courtly conduct, either is indicated to be a first step in the evolution of the relationship or is shown to be unsatisfying in the long run.

Grimalte also engages in a confusing interplay of ideal "real" and real "real." He believes in being the courtly lover, and his frequent invocation of *coplas* (although he is not the only poet in the work) in order to strengthen a point attests to this attitude. Gradissa is shown to yield to the persuasive power of Fiometa's prose. Grimalte, at the

---

[8] Strife was seen as the chief cause of social decay. Fifteenth-century Spain saw a revival of the belief in the system of patronage as a resolution to social strife. Love, even though it is itself a contrary, contradictory force, was viewed as the opposite of discord. Therefore, it is not surprising to find a correlation between the poetry and the social reality, both of which encouraged a system of patronage. See especially, "Traditional Forms of Patronage," pp. 53-66, in Chapter 2 of *The Troubadour Revival: A Study of Social Change and Traditionalism in Late Medieval Spain* (London: Routledge and Kegan Paul, 1978).

end, abandons his active pursuit of Gradissa in order to imitate a different reality, that of Pamphilo's behavior. Pamphilo has become a savage in the wilderness and, after searching for twenty-seven years and finally locating him in Asia, Grimalte decides to emulate the nearly-unrecognizable Pamphilo.

It is my contention in this study that a major point of the sentimental romances of violent love is to show the inherent flaw in the courtly code. That is to say, the imitation of this code in reality is not viable. *Cancionero* love poetry functions in a very limited manner: the poems are static lamentations about the ravages of love and the poets claim that these lamentations are the consequence of real experience. It is my belief that, as a genre, the sentimental romances of violent love are meant to be works of *reprobatio amoris*, not just in a moral way, but simply for survival: love brings with it disaster. What sets *Grimalte y Gradissa* apart from the other works examined thus far is that we see actual readers realizing the dangers of love, as Weissberger tells us:

> It has gone generally unremarked that the four principal characters of the work are not only lovers and beloveds, as their literary tradition demands, but that they are also newly conscious of themselves and each other as authors, readers, and characters of books. This type of self-consciousness is unprecedented in Castilian prose fiction... It suggests that, like his contemporary San Pedro, Juan de Flores incorporated into his second romance an awareness of himself as producer and of his public as excited consumers of an extraordinary new commodity—the printed book. (p. 65)

Weissberger is correct that the focus of *Grimalte* is on reading, or, at least, on types of literary creation, but she emphasizes too strongly that it is this particular text that occasions the interplay of fiction and literature. Indeed, all the works under consideration in this study occasion an interplay of literature and life, albeit in varying degrees.[9]

The importance of Weissberger's article is that she details Flores' weavings of characters who read about other characters and who know that they, too, will appear as characters, if for no other reason than that there is such an insistence that everything be written down. In the other sentimental romances the suggestion often made in the prologue is that the particular story could, or even better, would

---

[9] In the final chapter of this study, I discuss the interplay of literature and life in the Spanish sentimental romances.

encourage the reader or listener to remember and heed whatever the particular lesson was that was contained in the subsequent narrative.

Weissberger's study is important also for the associations she makes between fiction and reality by comparing Cervantes' treatment in *Don Quijote* and Flores' much earlier one in *Grimalte y Gradissa*. But the linkage of literature and life in *Don Quijote* differs from that of *Grimalte y Gradissa* in a way not mentioned by Weissberger. In *Grimalte y Gradissa*, fiction itself is not an issue for the characters, however much an issue it may be for us as readers, as it is in *Don Quijote*. However we choose to view Flores and judge the cleverness of his playing with fiction and reality, it seems important to recall that, for the characters within *Grimalte y Gradissa*, there is no doubt that those people who are subjects of written texts really existed, because they later show up as contemporary characters in the work. Flores chooses to respect the illusion that Fiammetta is the author of her own story not just because he was to bring her into his own story as a "real" character, but because all these love stories were seen as truthful accounts of happy or, more frequently, woeful experiences. In *Don Quijote* there is often a more decided separation of fiction from real life, which someone like the Canon of Toledo realizes, although Don Quijote himself may not. In *Grimalte y Gradissa* there is no one who stands up to label Fiometa's story, or anyone else's, a fiction, since it is all considered to be real.

*Reason and Will and the Use of Verse in "Grimalte y Gradissa"*

That women are creatures of passion and not of reason was Torrellas' contention in *Grisel y Mirabella*. Braçayda did not disagree with this judgment; in fact, she concurred and responded by placing more responsibility squarely on the men. She felt that they should, through their superior dominance of reason, reject the advances made by women. In *Grimalte y Gradissa*, another pair of lovers finds itself caught up in the same dichotomy of reason versus will:

> The... point that is made repeatedly is that men are more rational creatures than women, particularly in their behaviour in love. This is, of course, not the view which is conveyed by the love poetry of the *cancioneros*, but one more readily acceptable from the author of Torrellas' views on women in *Grisel y Mirabella* and the creator of the post-Boccaccio Pamphilo...

Pamphilo and Fiometa are shown behaving respectively according to *razón* and to *voluntad* as Flores conceives them. The claims of reason are pressed in vain on Fiometa on the various occasions when Grimalte tries to console her for Pamphilo's coldness.[10]

The topics of *razón* and *voluntad* are developed in *Grimalte y Gradissa* not only through the actions of the characters, but by what they say in their conversations and in their oral verse. The poetry in *Grimalte* is a problematic feature. In Waley's opinion:

> The verses used in *Grimalte* are not easy to account for in terms of artistic and technical effectiveness... They add nothing to the narrative or the subject matter and have little poetic merit, and the fact that they were written not by Flores but by Alonso de Córdoba, of whom no other writings are known, would seem to make them alien to the conception of the novel were it not that each verse or set of verses is introduced in the course of the prose text. (p. lvi)

What seems important here, and Waley herself mentions it, is precisely that Flores introduces the verses within the prose text. In fact, Flores melds the prose and verse so that it is part of each character's speech and, as we will see, each character's personality, especially with regard to their individual perceptions of reason and will.

When Pamphilo pleads with Fiometa to abandon her ardent pursuit of him, he appeals to her reason in order that she recognize that her honor is at stake:

> Y dexaste tu noble marido y tal senyoria y casa qual ninguna ygual de ti conozco. Pues ¿como sera posible que persona de tal estado pueda con stranyo hombre en agenas tierras bevir sin que tus parientes y amigos no hayan de proveher sobre ti? Que si tu con el amor demasiado te plaze perder honor, los otros no lo quieren. Pero que bien es que seas liberal en aquello que a ti solamente te toca, mas que tu hagas mercedes de la honor de muchos es grande agravio, por cierto. Pienso que quadauno de la perdida tuya le alcança parte.[11]

Fiometa remains unconvinced, and continues her verbal and written supplications. Pamphilo responds with more threats of the future disasters which could be attributed to lost honor. More specifically, he speaks of the conflict between reason and desire, as in these remarks to Grimalte, who has come in hopes of persuading Pamphilo to rekindle his devotion to Fiometa:

[10] Waley, "Love and Honour in the *Novelas sentimentales* of Diego de San Pedro and Juan de Flores," *BHS*, 43 (1966), 253-75, p. 272.

[11] Juan de Flores, *Grimalte y Gradissa*, ed. Pamela Waley (London: Tamesis, 1971), p. 21. All quotations from *Grimalte y Gradissa* will be from this edition.

Las cosas agenas se suelen dessear, y depues que son ya suyas, de quien las pide son en si quasi en nada tenidas...Que esto es cosa comuna, que quan presto desseamos, tan presto avorrecemos; y aquello que todos hazeys, quereys que a mi solo culpe, siendo la pena vulgar...Mas lo que las voluntades dessean no deve hombre hazerlo todo. (pp. 28-29)

When women have been attained, Pamphilo continues, it is dangerous for them: "Todas ellas, antes que se vienen al querer de los hombres que las requieren, estan en su entera discrecion, y entonçes los hombres la pierden; y despues ya de vencidas, pierden su buen iuyzio, quando ellos lo ganan" (p. 29).

Fiometa still refuses to relinquish her hopes of a reconciliation, but vows that her death is near: "Mi fin es venida/con graves tormientas/ Mas no que tu sientas/Del mal de mi vida" (p. 34). Pamphilo then moves from the examples of her shame on earth to the potential loss of heaven:

Y si de ti no te dueles, duelete de la honra de de tu marido, el qual ahun queda en el mundo por memoria de perdurable desonra, la qual mas que la muerte mata. Despierta pues el nuevo iuizio, y torna a cobrar tu vida. no des lugar que mueran las tuyas y agenas honras. Pues claro esta que tus desordenados desseos ningun remedio merecen, ni del cielo venirte puede, si tus obras no se meioran, pues ya tu merecimiento es iniusto. Pienso agora que los hombres, ahun que affeccion los sigue, seguimos mas a razon que a los deleytes de la voluntad. (p. 35)

Pamphilo sums up his argument in a poem to Fiometa, in which he emphasizes the potential loss of heaven:

O desonrada, perdida,
Que ya viviendo te lloro,
Remedia sobre tu vida,
que vale mas que thesoro.

Si piensas en lo perdido
Que ya no puedes cobrar,
Te sera causa de olvido
Para mi, sin desear.

Este conseio te do
Para tu bien infinito,
Porque vivas como yo

> Que de amor so libre y quito.
> Que volverme a tu desseo
> Y vençerme de tu guerra,
> Antes yo presumo y creo
> Que el cielo se torne tierra. (pp. 36-37)

Pamphilo's belated concern for his own soul as well as that of Fiometa seems genuine. He employs poetry as a means of providing counsel for Fiometa and self-justification to Grimalte through the espousal of reason. Before Fiometa's suicide, poetry was for Pamphilo not an emotional experience nor the crystallization of his thoughts in an aesthetic manner, but an effective means (or so he hoped) of convincing Fiometa to leave him alone and repent of her sinful ways:

> Y por senyal y memoria que de ti misma te miembres y a mi olvidar procures, por esta copla que en fin de aquesta te enbio, te lo quiero asi pedir y requiero;
> Olvida, olvida, olvidada,
> Olvida, pues yo te olvido.
> ........................
> Olvida, pues, lo querido,
> Que quieres do no te quieren
> Qu'es un dolor scondido,
> Con que tus gozos se mueren. (pp. 22-23)

Having pleaded with her directly by letter and through the intervention of Grimalte, without any result, Pamphilo goes with Grimalte to the monastery where Fiometa is waiting. They plead with each other to see the other's point of view. Pamphilo moves from a persuasive conversation to poetry, which he intends that Fiometa read: "Y porque mas affeccion de lo a ti complidera me quede, lo que scrivo te quiero por otra nueva invencion conseiar con avisos de lo que cumple que hagan, bien amar a ti y olvidar a mi. Son las coplas quales leyendo sentiras; y concluyo: O desonrada, perdida..." (p. 36).

In his final argument to Fiometa, the one which drives her to suicidal despair, Pamphilo is completely exasperated:

> Por esto me pareçe ser ya vicio mas despender palabras contigo, pues a ti ninguna buena razon puede satisfazerte, ni menos a ti tus desseos contentar, que no podria tan fuera de mis sentidos estar en que ellos consienta. Vive desto segura, si vida ayudarte puede, que mas los dissolutos males en el ageno lecho cometer no

me veras. Porque casos hay que hahun que la voluntad los pide, la
virtud los avorrece; y esto ya mi corazon muy affirmado lo tiene,
y en esto no creas ninguna mudança me puede enpeescer. (p. 41)

He recognizes that verse has a different value from that of prose, or
he would not have bothered to use it at all, but this recognition is
never more evident than within this final speech to Fiometa.
Whereas before his verse was to be read in a letter, he hopes here
that the hearing of it may produce on Fiometa the desired effect. it
is the ultimate weapon of persuasion:

Y pues veo que mis razones y cartas ante ti no pueden nada
acabar, quiero trocar el stilo en otra nueva manera, porque creo
que mas dulçemente dicho enganyare tus oydos para que por las
puertas de aquellos entren dos otras coplas a tus sentidos. (p. 42)

Grimalte's challenge to Pamphilo to a duel for the avenging of
Fiometa's death is answered by Pamphilo's letter telling of his own
sorrow and decision to do penance by exiling himself to live with
the "brutos animales." His letter to Grimalte ends with an apostro-
phe to the world: "¡O mundo desventurado/con caducos gualar-
dones,/De quien mas es prosperado/Tiene mayores passiones!" (p.
60).

By the time Grimalte reaches Pamphilo's father's palace, Pamphilo has made good his promise to disappear into the wilderness.
When Grimalte finally encounters the savage Pamphilo, the latter is
tearfully joyful over the devotion and diligence Grimalte has shown
in his search. His final poem is a summation of his conversation
with Grimalte—the conflict within him between gratitude for having a companion and knowing that this companion brings reminders
of past deeds and renewed sorrow: "Esforçat, angustia mia,/Esforçat
con mas dolor,/Que la nueva companyia/Es gualardon de la amor."
(p. 70).

For Pamphilo, then, poetry was a means of persuading Fiometa
to reconsider her desires. He states at one point that he adds verse
as a last resort since she has ignored the advice in his letters and in
his verbal confrontations with her. Once she is dead, however,
Pamphilo's two final poems are emotional releases: the one, an
apostrophic lamentation of the world's deceptions, the other an
exclamation of anguish, that love has provided him with a companion (Grimalte) to remind him of his pain. His use of poetry
changes from a philosophical stance, in which he projects his ideas
towards someone, to one in which poetry serves in the outpouring

of emotion. In the latter case, his use of poetry is more like that of Grimalte.

Pamela Waley was the first to mention that much of the narrative, contrary to the title, is the story of two other lovers, Pamphilo and Fiometa. In terms of sheer quantity of words devoted to these two lovers, Waley's observation is certainly true. But what we have seen in the other sentimental romances is the primary importance of man's imitative nature and the destructive nature of desire. As I have mentioned before, love service itself, as a code of known rules of conduct, inspires and requires imitation. The story of Grimalte and Gradissa is not so much the detailing of their love affair as it is their respective means of imitation. For both Grimalte and Gradissa, imitation is a primary factor for their actions. At first, they are involved in a courtly relationship which began before the opening actions of the book. Gradissa's incitement to action by the reading of Fiometa's autobiography is imitative to the extent that she cautions her own lover, Grimalte, that their future depends on the outcome of the hoped-for reconciliation of Pamphilo and Fiometa. The scope of their relationship has become enlarged by the added dimension of two more characters' fates relating to their own. Weissberger's description of Gradissa as reader is apt:

> The heroine of *Grimalte* is thus characterized first and foremost as an exceedingly empathetic reader of sentimental fiction; only secondarily is she presented as the kind of honor-bound "belle dame sans merci" portrayed by all of her predecessors . . . It is not the courtly code but Gradissa's own impassioned reading of romance that conditions her behavior towards her lover . . . .In the character of Gradissa, Flores presents a clear case—the earliest in Spanish literature—of *incitación* by means of the written word, to borrow Américo Castro's famous term for the effects of reading *libros de caballerías* on Alonso Quijano. (pp. 68-69)

In terms of their poetry, Gradissa is similar to Pamphilo before Fiometa's suicide. She offers only two poems, one in conversation at the opening of the work, the other near the end in a letter to Grimalte. For Gradissa, verse is a practical means of summing up her conditions for Grimalte's love service. Her practicality comes through in the preamble to the poem which concludes her conversation. We see that Gradissa views love service as a sort of business deal: "Y pues, ya vedes que en tomar este trabaio por mi es el precio con que me haveys de comprar, y quanto mas la paga se tardare, tanto mas sera detener vuestros desseos" (pp. 5-6). Poetry has a practical use as a device to jog the memory:

> Y porque lo metrificado mas dulcemente atrahe a los sentidos a recebir la memoria, alende de lo informado, por esta mi cancion lo quiero mas refirmar assi:
>> Si quereys este bien mio,
>> Cobrarlo como quereys,
>> Hit alla do vos enbio,
>> Y fazet quanto podreys. (p. 6)

Gradissa's other poetic contribution is a curt summation of her displeasure at the way Grimalte has handled the matter of Pamphilo and Fiometa, especially in permitting Pamphilo to go free after Fiometa's death:

>> Los desseos alcançados
>> Del amor y sus memorias
>> Queden los muy desseados
>> Sin parte de aquellas glorias.

>> Y pues esto os satisfaze,
>> Para comun estamiento
>> Yo os digo que no me plaze
>> De vuestro contentamiento. (p. 63)

Of the two lovers, Grimalte and Gradissa, she is the one more readily associated with *razón*. She is affected by what she reads, but in exactly the way the authors of sentimental romances would have liked of their readers: she learns from what she reads. Gradissa is not adversely affected by Fiometa's tragic death—she learns from it. As she writes to Grimalte at the end of the work:

> Porque si ell [Pamphilo] sin castigo quedasse, ¿quien escarmentaria a vos? Y si agora yo me veo libre, ¿querriades vos que en las redes de aquella Fiometa me lançasse? Por cierto, en quanto pueda, foyre de caher en ellas. Y como Pamphilo pudo despedir aquella sin verguença, menos enpacho devo yo tener en despediros. (p. 63)

Gradissa chooses to be more as Pamphilo was before Fiometa's suicide: he is rational and he looks out for himself. Gradissa has chosen not to follow the literary model presented by the impulsive, passionate Fiometa, but to follow the real-life model of Pamphilo as the one who rejects the relationship because it may do her harm. In all her decisions she functions rationally, from the contract she initially makes with Grimalte, that the reconciliation of Pamphilo and Fiometa is the price with which he may attain her, to her most rational view that what had happened to one woman in love could well befall her if she permitted the relationship to continue.

Grimalte, on the other hand, represents *voluntad* throughout the entire work. He remains a courtly lover, albeit an unsuccessful one, for most of the story until he changes from being a follower of a ritualized and literary code to the follower of Pamphilo's true model of penitence. Grimalte, unlike Gradissa, carries the courtly service to the extreme, so that, if we are to believe the written account, his entire life has been, and will continue to be, affected by it: he has followed Pamphilo's trail for twenty-seven years and joined him in his lonely exile, although not for exactly the same reasons. Pamphilo suffered from his feelings of guilt over Fiometa's death. Grimalte failed in a courtly charge and suffers from the disintegration of his bond to Gradissa. There is a gap between the magnitude of Pamphilo's crime and the artificiality of Grimalte's failure, a distinction which would undoubtedly be recognized by the follower of *razón* in contradistinction to the follower of *voluntad*.

Initially, Grimalte is more closely identified with Fiometa, since he has come to her aid in the quest for Pamphilo. If Gradissa's approach to poetry is closer to the majority of Pamphilo's verses, we can see a similar connection between Grimalte and Fiometa, a similarity which is not surprising, since they represent the passionate, emotional halves of their respective couples.

Both Grimalte and Fiometa appear to recognize differences between prose and poetry, not just from the point of view that poetry can bring about a certain effect on the listener/reader. Both indicate an awareness of creating poetry, of intentionally producing something different, something literary. Their statements, which precede each poem, demonstrate this difference.

In Grimalte's case, for example, he distinguishes between the prose of Fiometa's autobiography and the poetry he recites:

> Alende desto haun me quiero atrever que si la prosa ha desde-nyado mi causa, que quiça que en corto rimo dire algo que bien hos parescera, tomando a vos [Fiometa, although at this point he is unaware of her real identity] por speio en que por cierta invencion se me descubre la siguiente cancion. (p. 13)

In a similar fashion, Fiometa, aware of the literary nature of her writings, precedes a long poem to Pamphilo with these words: "Y desto quiero, como supiere, componer o artizar algunos metros para meior testimonio de tus obras y las mias. Y dexando la prosa, a la copla asi me vengo" (p. 39). The poetry is a means of redefining and reaffirming the emotions expressed in the conversations that precede it. Because it is no more than a redefinition, it seems to be more contrived than the poetry of Gradissa and Pamphilo; it is less effective than the persuasive verse of Pamphilo or the practical verse of Gradissa. Both Grimalte and Fiometa often refer to their verse as "copla" and "canción," although Gradissa also calls her verse "canción."

The main difference is that the poetry of Gradissa and Pamphilo addresses specific issues, people, and a moment in time and, of primary importance, they pertain to the concept of *razón*. The verses of Grimalte and Fiometa are too literary, too "cancioneril." They could, with few if any exceptions, be found in any *cancionero*, referring to no historical incident in particular.

Fiometa's mode of poetry is static: lamentations are paralleled by angry accusations to Pamphilo for his hardheartedness and unwavering rejection of her. Grimalte, on the other hand, does confront horrible reality at one point and his poetry reflects it. When Fiometa comprehends that Pamphilo's rejection of her is final, Grimalte at first attempts to comfort her with platitudes about the common sorrows of love and the notion that time heals all wounds:

Y por ablandaros vuestro duro coraçon y amenguar algo de vuestro dolor, despues de mi disponer a lohor de vuestra honra y provar para quanto bastare mi sentido, mudando la habla en rimo:

Esfuerçat esfuerço fuerte
Contra las penas de amar,
Que la vida, sin la muerte,
Todo puede remediar.

Y si mal haveys tovido
De amores sin gradecer,
Procurat por el olvido
Que se suele aborrecer. (p. 51)

Grimalte is, at least, aware enough to realize that his words fall on deaf ears because Fiometa is really dying. When he takes in the truth that she is indeed dead, he does an about-face from his anterior poetry and laments her death in a realistic fashion:

¡O muerte desesperada,
Para mi que ya te spero!
Ven por mi, no tardes nada;
Pues eres tan desseada
Que mas que vida te quiero.
Dame complido morir
En este punto de agora,
Que no me plaze bevir
Depues de aquesta senyora. (p. 52)

*Reason and Will as Turning Point*

Fiometa's death represents the point in which each of the remaining characters will be faced with a choice: which to follow, *razón*
or *voluntad*? After constructing an elaborate sepulchre adorned with
his poetic creations, Grimalte lashes out at Pamphilo in a letter,
challenging him to accept the responsibility for Fiometa's death and
to fight a duel. What Grimalte objects to most, it seems, is the
reversal of what should be, and is, the norm, if one is to believe the
testimony of the *cancionero* verse, that men, not women, should die
of love; "Que cierto, si vuestros yerros mirays, de la muerte vos
seran causa. Pues pareçe que nuevas leyes usays en amor, en querer
y consentir que aquella tan sin errores assi moriesse por vos, que
mas razonable cosa es, como suele acaheçer, a nosotros hombres
morir por las mujeres" (p. 58).

Grimalte is completely mystified by what he considers to be
Pamphilo's new rules in love. He is able to persuade Pamphilo, who
was so firm in his belief that the affair should not begin again, by
using Pamphilo's own line of reasoning. Grimalte calls it "razonable
cosa" that men, not women, die from love.

Pamphilo refuses the challenge to a duel, but is persuaded to
accept responsibility for Fiometa's death. Again, the idea of reason
and, in this case, rightness, is expressed:

Mas no quiero mis scusas asi me dexen sin penitencia, mas pienso
y conociendo creo que menos tormento me seria morir una sola
vez, como muy muchas merezca, lo qual a mi no contenta ni
aquella mi satisfaze. Por esta causa me doy por vuestro vençido,
que cierto segun vuestra gran razon mi misma spada me seria la
matadora. (p. 59)

At this point, Pamphilo goes off to do penance and Grimalte
undertakes the unpleasant task of informing Gradissa of his failure.
I have mentioned already that Gradissa chooses not to continue the

relationship because she might become a victim as Fiometa did. She rejects love in order to follow reason: "Y porque vehays quanto me duele su muerte, deveys sin duda pensar que tan llagada me veo que me haze partir la voluntad de amores, las quales los alegres coraçones piden, mayormente quando a execucion llegan" (p. 63).

Grimalte could give up his quest and accept his failure in love but he does not. He turns his attention to seeking out Pamphilo in order to join him in his "desesperada empresa," hoping with this act to prove his intense, eternal loyalty to Gradissa. Typically, Grimalte ends his letter with a poem: "En esta triste partida;/Que me enbias,/ Feneceran con mi vida/Tus porfias" (p. 64). Comparing his quest to Jason's, Grimalte searches for Pamphilo, finally locating him after twenty-seven years. Pamphilo is completely transformed to a Wild Man, and the idea of reason is once again mentioned:

> Y depues que Pamphilo fue de la cueva sallido, quando le vi, de tan desfigurado facion stava que si no lo hoviera visto denante, ningun humano iuyzio lo podria a ninguna difformidad comparar. Porque todos los senyales de persona racional tenia perdidos por muchas razones. (p. 67)

Grimalte does not abandon his role as imitator, he expands it. Whereas before he imitated a code, expressed primarily in a literary way through the abundance of verse in the book, he now imitates a real person. In addition, whereas Grimalte's earlier imitations were of emotional, sentimental experiences, the imitation is amplified to include a manner of living which includes physical as well as mental degeneration. Grimalte self-indulgently calls himself the legitimate heir to Pamphilo's sufferings and states outright his desire to imitate Pamphilo:

> "E fuyme a lo mas spesso de aquell boscaie, adonde mis vestidos me despoie, y començe a tomar possession de aquell tan triste bevir y morada; y las manos puestas por el suelo en la manera que aquell andava, siquiendo sus pizadas, tomandolo por maestro de mi nuevo officio" (p. 69).

Together they continue in this life, being tormented by grotesque visions of Fiometa in flames, who is tortured by devils, and Grimalte continues his imitative behavior. A final and ironic linking of *voluntad* and *razón* occurs, followed immediately by another example of Grimalte's conscious choice to imitate Pamphilo:

> Y yo asi grande parte del dia stuve contemplando qual enemigo proposito a la vida tan desesperada me truxo. Y muchas vezes la

voluntad pensava que la religion tan estrecha renunciasse; mas mirado como no menor pena me daria la verguença de bolverme que el dolor de comportar la tan travaiosa penitencia, por esta razon me detuve, en special que en respecto de aquella tan triste vida que yo dexe, es muy piadosa la que tengo. A la qual poniendo muy buen coraçon, guarnido de suffrimiento, me haze por mas seguro suffrir este dolor. Y passados algunos dias en ell, ya como habituado assi como Pamphilo en las sus desaventuras me halle, tomando aquell refrigerio de las visiones ya dichas. Y como a cabo de dias me aquexo mantenimiento, veyendo que a Pamphilo las yervas solas le davan dulçe comer, no menos yo comence su verde gusto. (p. 73)

Grimalte claims that he would be giving in to will were he to renounce this activity, which he compares to a religious calling. It is ironic that Pamphilo's animal-like behavior is seen as reasonable, while the idea of returning to his former life would be an act of "voluntad." Grimalte would undoubtedly respond that the abandonment of this religious calling would be completely unacceptable. The narrative ends with a letter from Grimalte to Gradissa in which he blames her cruelty for his life of continual sorrow and penance and his impending death.

### Conclusion

The structure of Grimalte y Gradissa involves an interplay of writing and reading, the contrast of reason and will, and the idea of desire and non-desire.

On the level of writing, Flores initially confuses us by telling us that he is the protagonist of the work even though he has changed his name to Grimalte. Consequently, throughout the work we share Flores' thoughts from a temporal perspective as well as an actual one: ostensibly, he wrote of his adventures to Gradissa, and what we are reading is the story within the story, in which the narrator relates to us his adventures from an earlier time and his current perspective on them. The literary nature of the work is amplified by the major importance of the verse which ends almost every speech and letter, and by the inclusion of references to an earlier writing and the appearance of another author's literary figures as real people.

The confusion of literature and life is exemplified by the conflict provoked: dealing with desire through the examination of, and application of, either reason or will.   One problem, as Flores shows us, is that the characters have individual interpretations of reality; consequently, their acknowledgments of reason and will conform to their particular world view. This idea can be illustrated by comparing an image connected with three characters, all having to do with perceptions of Fiometa.

Each character speaks of a mirror, albeit metaphorically. Now, a mirror, unlike a painting, for example, normally renders an unaltered reflection of what exists before it. Gradissa says, when she explains Grimalte's quest to him:

> Hos pido que todas las cosas que entre ella y su Pamphilo passaran por extenso scritas me las envjeys, porque yo vea el fin que de la amor reciben aquellos que suyos son. Y vos trebaiat que Fiometa le aya tal y tan prospero que yo me desee ser ella; y si lo contrario, lo que Dyos no quiera acaheciesse, seria a mi contado a ignorancia que, viendome libre, a lo semejante me offreciesse. Assi que ella me sera un speio de doctrina con que vea lo que con vos me cumple hazer. (p. 5)

Grimalte, while recounting the nature of his search to the woman who has not let it be known that she is indeed Fiometa, is inspired to compose a poem:

> Alende desto haun me quiero atraver que si la prosa ha desde- nyado mi causa, que quiça que en corto rimo dire algo que bien hos parescera, tomando a vos por speio en que por cierta inven- cion se me descubre la siguiente cancion:
>
>> Si mis terribles enoios
>> Quieren mi muerte vençida,
>> Vuestra beldat y mis oios
>> Han remediado mi vida. (p. 13)

Finally, Pamphilo, after having tried to convince Fiometa that she was in spiritual danger, reverts again to the idea of honor. Since Fiometa will not consider her own honor nor that of her husband, Pamphilo hopes that his own stance of being both the repentant lover and reasonable man will serve as a model for Fiometa: "Pero lo que contigo acabar podria es atraherte con el speio de honor. ¡Quanto muy mas obligado te soy agora que quando con nuevos oios y corazon encendido tus amores procurava!" (pp. 41-42).

For Gradissa, whose practicality and ability to maintain the use of reason is stressed throughout the work, Fiometa is "speio de doctrina." The courtly love affair is, for Gradissa, no mere social pastime: Fiometa's autobiography and her subsequent actions serve as doctrine, an unwavering guideline. Fiometa is the unwitting mediator of Gradissa's final stance of non-desire. Gradissa avoids the pitfalls of mimetic desire and shows herself to be the ideal moral reader, one who benefits from the example of another's misfortune.

Grimalte, on the other hand, permits himself to be affected by Fiometa's beauty, a beauty which inspires him to immediate poetic creativity. That Grimalte consistently views reality with one eye to the literary code is obvious even in this instance. He is forced to set aside his ideal—the courtly code—in order to deal with a new mediator, the printed book, but he never completely abandons that ideal.

Pamphilo's words imply that he, too, was once so affected by Fiometa's beauty that he became passionately consumed with desire. Having renounced that way of life, he hopes to reverse the process, in which he drew passion from her beauty, so that she can, this time, see honor in him and draw upon that virtue in order to restore her own lost honor.

Fiometa uses no mirror and admits no reality but that which she infers from her own emotions and desires. While it is important to see *Grimalte y Gradissa* as the story of two couples, it is even more important to see that Fiometa is the central figure, whose actions and passions provide the impetus for everything that the other characters do. In other words, even though Fiometa is the only one driven to a physical death, her unyielding desire for Pamphilo causes the spiritual and physical degeneration of the men who cared for her.

Pamphilo and Grimalte are not blameless: Pamphilo pays with his life in exile for having committed adultery with Fiometa and for driving her to suicide; Grimalte self-indulgently permits himself to become a double of Pamphilo, living in exile to pay for Fiometa's death and to prove his loyalty to Gradissa. Gradissa, the only person who escapes death and exile, is the only one who consistently applies reason in the case of love and does not permit herself to be governed strictly by emotions, either in desire or in remorse.

As in *Grisel y Mirabella*, no generalizations can be made about either men or women. In fact, what Flores shows here is that the lines drawn by the characters in their speeches—that women are governed by emotions, men by reason—are utterly specious. While Gradissa, the consistent mouthpiece of reason, was like Pamphilo for part of the time, it is Pamphilo who then changes and becomes more like Grimalte.

Thus we see that in *Grimalte y Gradissa* Flores manages to confuse and undercut what he sets up. The men do not maintain reason as a guideline as much as they preach it, but fall prey to the emotions, which they manifest in mimetic desire and other forms of imitative behavior. Fiometa does live up to the worst view of women, but Gradissa clearly does not. The final lesson is that no good can come from love itself, but occasionally, in these matters, reason can overcome will, as evidenced by the very practical Gradissa.

# 5

# Juan de Segura's

## *Processo de cartas de amores*

## and *Luzindaro y Medusina:*

## Return to the Prototype

"Vençen el seso los dulçes errores,
mas non duran sienpre segund luego plazen;
pues me fizieron del mal que vos fazen,
sabed al amor desamar, amadores."
MACÍAS, in *Laberinto de Fortuna,* stanza 106

HE APPEARANCE IN 1548 of Juan de Segura's work, lengthily entitled *Processo de cartas de amores que entre dos amantes pasaron, con una carta del autor para un amigo suyo, pidiéndole consuelo y Quexa y aviso de un caballero llamado Luzindaro contra Amor y una dama y sus casos, con deleitoso estilo de proceder hasta el fin de ambos; sacado del estilo griego en nuestro castellano,* seems to be an anachronism, and, paradoxically, the innovator of a literary genre, the epistolary novel.[1] The first part

---

[1] *Processo de cartas* is the first prose work to be written in complete epistolary fashion, but it can in no way be considered a novel, although its imitators may indeed be novels. Rather it is a romance of frustrated love. I analyze the use of anachronism in this work, and Segura's awareness of Renaissance literary theory, in a forthcoming article "Anachronism in the work of a 'Careless' Counterfeiter: The Case of Juan de Segura."

of Segura's work, *Processo de cartas*, consists of forty letters between two lovers, a lamentation by the male protagonist, and four letters seeking and giving consolation. Menéndez y Pelayo was the first to suggest its innovatory nature, and his view was later confirmed by Kany in his study of the epistolary novel.[2] More often than not, the second part of the work, the romance *Luzindaro y Medusina*, is forgotten by the critics. Called an "appended novelette" by Edwin Place, the only modern critic to undertake a critical edition of Segura's work, *Luzindaro y Medusina* is not even included in his edition and translation of *Processo de cartas*.[3]

Unfortunately for *Luzindaro y Medusina* and its author, this neglect

---

[2] Menéndez y Pelayo said (*Orígenes de la novela* [1907; rpt. Madrid: CSIC, 1943], II, p. 67): "Creemos que Juan de Segura fue el primero entre los modernos que escribió una novela entera en cartas, generalizando el procedimiento que habían empleado ocasionalmente Eneas Silvio, Diego de San Pedro y aun otros autores más antiguos, como el poeta provenzal autor de *Frondino y Brissona*." Charles E. Kany corroborated Menéndez y Pelayo's theory in *The Beginnings of the Epistolary Novel in France, Italy and Spain*, University of California Publications in Modern Philology, 21, part 1 (Berkeley: University of California Press, 1937), p. 72: "Although the work contains many letters that teem with extravagant conceits of the time, it is nevertheless of great importance in the development of the genre, for it is the first modern novel made up entirely of letters. Juan de Segura, having generalized the procedure of Aeneas Sylvius, Diego de San Pedro, and even older authors, has thus honored the literature of Spain. Save for its mention in histories of Spanish literature, Spain's claim to priority in the epistolary novel has never been sufficiently recognized." See especially chapters 2 and 3 for a discussion of the Spanish antecedents to European epistolary fiction from the fourteenth to the sixteenth centuries.

[3] Juan de Segura, *Processo de cartas de amores: A Critical and Annotated Edition of this First Epistolary Novel (1548) together with an English Translation*, ed. and trans. Edwin B. Place, Northwestern University Studies, Humanities Series, 23 (Evanston, Illinois: Northwestern University Press, 1950). I have used this edition when quoting from *Processo de cartas* since it is the best modern edition. Both Place and Joaquín del Val agree that *Luzindaro y Medusina* appeared with *Processo de cartas* in the first edition, but it is missing from the surviving copy. However, *Luzindaro y Medusina* survives in the Venetian edition of 1553, which Joaquín del Val reproduces (Sociedad de Bibliófilos Españoles, 31 [Madrid, 1956]) along with the other contents of that MS, *Cartas de refranes* of Blasco de Garay and Cristobal de Castillejo's *Diálogo de mujeres*. I have used this edition when quoting from *Luzindary y Medusina*. The work attached to *Processo de cartas* is usually referred to as *Quexa y aviso*, but because I deal with so many romances and amorous pairs with similar names, I have found it helpful to be reminded of the names as often as possible in order to avoid confusion with the other works.

exemplifies one of the ironies of literary criticism since *Processo de cartas*, the only part to receive any critical attention, was not very popular, while the "appended novelette" went through six dozen editions in France in the second half of the sixteenth century alone.[4] *Luzindaro y Medusina* has been eclipsed not by the superior content and theme of *Processo de cartas*, but by its format. The realism of the epistolary section of the work as a whole is more respected than the part Menéndez y Pelayo disdained in his *Orígenes de la novela*.[5] Such a judgment falls readily into the critical frame admired by the nineteenth-century critics. As Alban Forcione tells us, speaking specifically about the critical reception of Cervantes' *Persiles*:

> The past one hundred years have not been so kind to the *Persiles*...
> Among Cervantists detractors have outnumbered admirers of the
> work, and even the latter have insisted on viewing it with nine-
> teenth-century literary values in mind, redeeming the second half
> of the work for its "realism" while scoring the fantastic excesses of
> the first half... Thus, the "two Cervantes" of Menéndez y Pelayo,
> the one aspiring to the impossible realms of the ideal and the
> fantastic—the world of the *Galatea*, the *Persiles*, and the "idealistic"
> novella—the other preoccupied with the flow of real, human ex-
> perience and possessed of a keen critical faculty which inexorably
> cut short his flights into fantasy, the Cervantes of *Don Quijote* and
> the "realistic" novella.[6]

The two parts of Segura's work represent just such a combination,

[4] *Processo de cartas* had four editions in Spain (Kany, p. 72) while *Luzindaro y Medusina* was much more popular in France as well as in Spain (Joaquín del Val, p. xl). Regarding the ironies of literary analysis, Keith Whinnom cites the tendency of critics to "rescue" works of art spurned by their audience while disparaging others which met with great success. He suggests that, perhaps, in our zeal to discover great literature we are finding pearls where none exists and, in the second case, applying critical criteria which either had no contemporary relevance or simply were not the goal of the works studied. For these and other points of warning to the critic, see *Spanish Literary Historiography: Three Forms of Distortion* (Exeter: University, 1967). See also his article, "The Problem of the 'Best-Seller' in Spanish Golden Age Literature," *BHS*, 57 (1980), 189-98.

[5] Speaking about *Luzindaro y Medusina*, Menéndez y Pelayo says: "Es una extraña mezcla de discursos sentimentales, alegorías confusas y gran copia de aventuras fantásticas; en lo cual se distingue de todos los demás libros de su género, asimilándose mucho más a los de caballerías y aun a las novelas orientales," *Orígenes*, p. 68.

[6] Alban K. Forcione, *Cervantes' Christian Romance: A Study of "Persiles y Sigismunda"* (Princeton: University Press, 1972) p. 3.

the "realistic" experience of the epistolary section and the fantastic, allegorical, sentimental, and chivalric section on the two lovers, Luzindaro and Medusina. Joaquín del Val, the only critic to provide us with an edition of *Luzindaro y Medusina*, did not believe that Segura was the author of this part, especially in view of the vast differences in the styles and content of the two works. Since this second part did appear in the first edition of the work and, since, as I hope to demonstrate, there are thematic similarities as well as stylistic ones between the two works, there is no concrete reason to suspect that del Val's judgment is correct, especially considering that the same kind of relationship is found in other sentimental romances, most notably *Siervo libre de amor*.[7]

The relationship between the prologue, *Processo de cartas*, and *Luzindaro y Medusina* is a curious one which establishes, and then confuses, boundaries of narrative voice. The prologue, from Juan de Segura to one Galeazzo Rótulo Osorio, "my master," falls clearly within the Renaissance mode of the defense and justification of what may be called pleasurable literature. Citing Greek and Latin writers in general, and the ultimate critical authority, Aristotle in particular, Juan de Segura defends his right to provide the public with yet another trite love story on the grounds that it will indeed edify, and furthermore, that he has been persuaded by many to undertake this venture. He claims to have translated the work from Greek:

> Y como de muchos fuesse importunado que traduxesse esta obra del griego en castellano, determiné de ponerme al peligro de la furiosa opinión del vulgo, quiriendo antes dél ser con ponçoñosas reprehensiones mordido que vsar de ingratitud—vicio tan abominable—no cumpliendo lo que a vuestra merced deuía siguiendo su voluntad, que es que diesse pregón en público de mi ynocencia. (p. 30)

Certainly the questions concerning the literary theory of the Renaissance are important ones, although it is not my intention to

---

[7] I discuss more completely in the final chapter of this study structural and thematic characteristics of the Spanish sentimental romance. Armando Durán (*Estructura y técnicas de la novela sentimental y caballeresca*[Madrid: Gredos, 1973], p. 46) notices a connection between *Processo de cartas de amores* and *Luzindaro y Medusina* that is similar to the relationship between *Siervo libre de amor* and *Estoria de dos amadores*, but he fails to consider properly the significance of this by enforcing his too-rigorous schema for the sentimental romances, a schema criticized earlier in Chapter II.

discuss them here in detail.[8] What is important, however, is that
Segura firmly establishes in his prologue that the work which follows
is not a fiction and, in order to further reduce his complicity in the
boom of frivolous literature, states that he himself did not write it but
translated it from the Greek original. That it is from Greek literature
gives it more credibility, placing it more solidly among the acceptable
fictions of the time, those of unimpeachable didactic authority.[9]

In *Processo de cartas*, Juan de Segura identifies himself with the
narrative "I" of the letters written by the male lover, Captivo. In
letter 44, the heading is: "Carta de Ju. de Sa. para su leal amigo, Ho.
Orz., pidiéndole consuelo sobre sus amores" (p. 88). If, in fact, the "I"
of the prologue is also the "I" of the letters, then Segura is deceiving
the reader—intentionally? If nothing else, the epistolary exchange
between Ho. Orz., the friend, and Captivo serves as a distancing
device between the first part, *Processo de cartas*, and the third-person
narrative, *Luzindaro y Medusina*, which also contains some laments in
first person, dialogue, some love poetry of the type found in the
*cancioneros* and some of the other sentimental romances, and two
stanzas from Juan de Mena's *Laberinto de Fortuna*.[10] The entire work

---

[8] For a general discussion of Renaissance literary theory, see William
Nelson, *Fact or Fiction: The Dilemma of the Renaissance Storyteller* (Cambridge, MA:
Harvard University Press, 1973). For a discussion pertinent to Peninsular
Spanish literature, see Alban K. Forcione, *Cervantes, Aristotle and the "Persiles"*
(Princeton: University Press, 1970), pp. 3-87.

[9] Both Nelson (*Fact or Fiction*) and Forcione (*Cervantes, Aristotle, . . .*) discuss the
Greek revival in the literature of the Renaissance, from the fictional imitations
of Heliodorus to the debates over the classical aesthetic.

[10] The poetry in *Luzindaro y Medusina* merits a separate study. Of the ten
poems contained in the tale, two are attributed to Mena and are spoken by
Luzindaro, who states that he is quoting Macías. None of the other poems has
a heading; they are ostensibly the invention of Luzindaro. The two poems
headed "Mena" come from two stanzas of Juan de Mena's *Laberinto de Fortuna* and
are indeed spoken by Macías. Juan de Mena's popularity in the sixteenth
century is well known. As Florence Street explains in "Hernán Núñez and the
Earliest Printed Editions of Mena's *El laberinto de Fortuna,*" *MLR*, 61 (1966), 51-63:
"It is well known that the works of Juan de Mena enjoyed a quite sensational
success in the fifteenth and sixteenth centuries. In particular, his longest poem,
*El laberinto de Fortuna*, was printed over and over again," p. 51. See also María
Rosa Lida de Malkiel, *Juan de Mena: poeta del prerrenacimiento español*, Publicaciones
de la *NRFH*, 1 (Mexico City: El Colegio de México, 1950) and Otis H. Green,
"Juan de Mena in the Sixteenth Century: Additional Data," *HR*, 21 (1953), 138-
40.

ends with a poem warning of the dangers of earthly love and advocating the contemplation of the divine.

However, before it is possible to come to any conclusions about why Segura would combine such different narrative forms in one work, some general links between the two parts should be examined.

*Similarities of Theme and Imagery in "Processo de cartas" and "Luzindaro y Medusina"*

While the first part of the work, *Processo de cartas*, is a story of desire which is not satisfied, the second part, *Luzindaro y Medusina*, is one of desire satisfied, but ultimately ending in death. In this respect, Segura's work is in perfect accord with the other texts examined in this study, in that both parts exhibit the duality of love seen in the romances of Flores, San Pedro and Rodríguez del Padrón: a combination of violent love and frustrated love.

*Luzindaro y Medusina* is filled with elegant expressions and beautiful imagery. Structurally not as complex as other sentimental romances, *Luzindaro y Medusina* nevertheless blends rather successfully Renaissance and medieval elements, along with standard romance patterns and motifs. The wheel of Fortune, for example, which was a great preoccupation of medieval man, is often mentioned here as the cause of love's going awry. The medieval tradition of love service is exalted and is, in fact, the basis on which Descanso brings together Luzindaro and Medusina: Luzindaro, like Macías (who is cited in the text), is "un perfecto amador" (p. 93). Alongside such evocations of medieval fortune and the allegorical depictions of Descanso and Cupido, are found elements more typical of the Renaissance, such as emphasis on imagery of music and art, and on the notion of light as a symbol of man's reason.

*Luzindaro y Medusina*, which is mainly a story of violent love, begins with a shorter tale of frustrated love, the story of Garinaldo and Medusina. Garinaldo, the lover who travels to find Medusina, is thwarted by the sorceress Actelasia, who tells him that Medusina is dead. Stunned and heartbroken by the news, Garinaldo, we are told, lives out his life in sadness: "El apasionado amador, cuando esto oyó, quedó tal como muerto, y no aguardando a que la sabia más le dixese, despidióse d'ella y se tornó a su reino, a donde vivió siempre en vida muy triste por lo que la sabia dicho le había" (p. 63).

Luzindaro is more successful, thanks to Actelasia's art and the intercession of Descanso with Cupido. But there is a structural similarity in that he, like Garinaldo before him, falls in love from afar, travels to the beloved, and is fooled by a false death. Fortune is with Luzindaro, however, and the lovers are united in marriage by Descanso, amid great celebrations.

The only somber note is sounded by the prophecy of Actelasia on the morning after the wedding:

> Y la mañana venida, Actelasia los comenzó a hablar desta manera: "Excelentes y soberanos príncipes: ya habréis visto todo lo que por vosotros pasado ha, y aunque por mi saber aquí habéis sido juntados del arte que veis, no penséis que estáis tan seguros de contino gozar de lo que habéis gozado; porque, cuando la blanca paloma perdiere su ser, entonces la gran Fénix comenzará a alimentarse de su ceniza, hasta que tenga compañía a la blanca paloma que aguardándole estará. Y porque esto vendrá como tengo dicho, no penséis que las cosas en un ser de contino puedan permanescer... Y como las cosas que de arriba ordenadas están se hayan de cumplir, no ha podido dexar de pasar lo pasado, y pues que así es, quiero como de mi hijo (pues que así os lo puedo llamar) ordenar lo que a vuestro descanso más tocare." (pp. 93-94)

The prophecy is fulfilled: Medusina dies, and blackbirds come and cover her body with flowers. Luzindaro sets fire to the flowers and the body and, when all is ashes, he sustains himself on the ashes alone, until he, too, dies.

The phoenix appears also in *Processo de cartas*, in reference to Captivo:

> Si el Phénix se torna ceniza, y della, según naturaleza, otro salir suele, no es de marauillar que, siendo tan vnico yo en el mundo en vuestro seruicio, siendo en viuos fuegos de amor por vuestra causa abrasado, salga de mi ceniza otro yo, según que agora me hallo de nueuo a la vida tornado con vuestras sabrosas razones, de las quales he colegido el soberano bien que, mi señora, me hazéys en quererme por vuestro esposo; o qual acepto con la mayor alegría que jamás mi coraçón nunca huuo. (p. 65)

The connections are striking: it is the only time the phoenix is mentioned in *Processo de cartas* and it is linked to the affirmative response to a marriage proposal. In *Luzindaro y Medusina*, as we have seen, it is the day after the marriage ceremony that Actelasia prophesies the demise of Luzindaro and Medusina. There is never a question of the inconstancy of their love, but rather of the inconstancy of order, as we perceive it to be or as we wish it to be, whether it be the movement of Fortune's will or some other force in the universe.

The certainty that one cannot change what is to occur, or what has been decreed, is voiced in *Processo de cartas* by Doña Juliana in a manner similar to that of Actelasia:

> Mas las cosas que de lo alto hordenadas están, es escusado nadie querellas euitar, assi que, señor, es justo que vuestra merced como católico crea que ninguna cosa es por mano de Dios hecha que no sea por mejor. Y puede ser que este caso tan arrebatado y tan fuera del gusto de amos a dos sea causa que con mayor breuedad se junten en su seruicio; que, pues la intención es tan buena y sancta, es impossible que aya mal fin. (p. 85)

In Doña Juliana's consolation, fortune is subservient to the will of God; in Actelasia's prophecy, we know only of Fortune's mutability, not God's will, but the same sentiment of the ordered and planned universe is expressed.

If the consolatory phrases of religious service offered by Doña Juliana are not enough (and indeed they are not, since they are followed immediately by the protagonist's long and self-pitying lamentation and his letter to his friend requesting sympathy), there is another reason why Captivo should refrain from grieving. The friend who sends him *Luzindaro y Medusina* has this to say:

> Visto en quánto la fortuna os auía subido, y sin perder nada de lo ganado, en quanto vuestra desdicha os ha baxado, como quien vuestras cosas, mi verdadero señor, en el ánima siente, no puedo sino gozar de lo vno y aguar con lágrimas de tristeza lo otro.
> ¿Qué bien puede ser mayor que el avida?
> ¿Qué mal puede venir que en gran parte le yguale? Ninguno. Luego, si el bien es ecessivo, éste no perdiéndose, qualquiera acidente, mi señor, que os venga de pesar, le auéys con vuestro ánimo generoso de sobrellevar; pues no discrepando de lo principal de la raýz y cimiento de vuestra gloria, todo lo acessorio es de poca importancia, que como de cosa poca no se deue de hazer caso dello. (pp. 89-90)

As an example of consolation, the story of Luzindaro and Medusina is sent to Captivo. Captivo feels that his love affair has been cut short and he is destined to a life of sadness. Garinaldo is his counterpart in *Luzindaro y Medusina*. Garinaldo and Medusina loved each other, but, because of the intervention of Actelasia, are forever kept apart. Servidora is kept from Luzindaro by her brothers. Luzindaro's story, however, could also have been that of Captivo, had Captivo and Servidora gone through with their marriage plans and been permitted to be reunited.

Both sections deal with literal and metaphorical captivity, as illustrated by the following diagram:

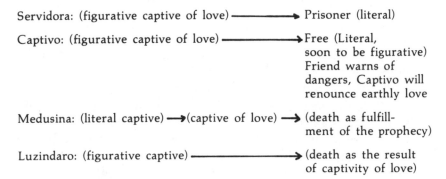

Servidora: (figurative captive of love) ⟶ Prisoner (literal)

Captivo: (figurative captive of love) ⟶ Free (Literal,
soon to be figurative)
Friend warns of
dangers, Captivo will
renounce earthly love

Medusina: (literal captive) ⟶(captive of love) ⟶ (death as fulfill-
ment of the prophecy)

Luzindaro: (figurative captive) ⟶ (death as the result
of captivity of love)

There is a strong hint of underlying disorder in *Luzindaro y Medusina* in contradistinction to the sense of rightness of their love which comes through in the tale. Even their names are significant. Luzindaro, containing the Spanish for light, moves from a metaphorical darkness (unrequited love and Medusina's false death and resurrection) to a metaphorical light (love and marriage) to a physical darkness (death). His reason is eclipsed by his will to love and he is led to his death. Medusina is a deceptively pretty name but is really "little Medusa." There is another reason to connect Medusina with Medusa—Luzindaro himself nearly does so. Amid railings against love, he compares passion to Medusa's venom:

> Estos son tus nombres: falso, engañador, que no manso y piadoso, señor de señores, rey de reyes; mas según yo llámote falso ciego de ciegos y cabeza de la ponzoñosa cabeza Medusea ¿qué te podré, enemigo mío, llamar? Que por más que trabaje en darte tu nombre, veo no poder de tu vergüenza concluir con el que mejor te cuadra, que es botica de pasión, donde las medicinas que de ti salen son ponzoñosas que das por remedios a los que al fin de su trabajo te piden descanso, y para dárselos abres un bote, y dales una medicina de color de tu color que es encarnado. (p. 65)

As the embodiment of human passion, Medusina's unenviable connection with Medusa is undeniable. Luzindaro's reliance on reason is no match for the desire sparked by the "serpent-woman." Lest we still disclaim the possibility of Medusina's darker side, the narrator later compares her lure to the legend of the virgin and the unicorn:

> Estando diciendo esto oyó un suave canto que mucho en su fuego de amor acrescentó. Y al sonido se fué a entrar en un vergel donde la suave melodía se hacía. Y andando por los cipreses y rosales (que muchos había) vió estar a su señora en un alto corredor, como de nuevo herida, cantando con una arpa en las manos, con tanta melodía, que como el unicornio, no viendo su muerte, se la paró a escuchar, estando por un rato adormescido. (p. 77)

The seeming innocence and beauty of such a scene is undermined by the reference to the unicorn's death, and by the well-known significance of that particular legend in folklore and literature.[11] While this kind of undermining does not occur in either *Processo de cartas* or *Luzindaro y Medusina* with the same frequency as in *Grisel y Mirabella*, for example, it is nevertheless true that in these works hints of disorder appear to show that love can be beautiful, but that it does have a violent side and that the rewards of love are few.

*Luzindaro y Medusina* ends with a strange, negative note on the theme of the loyal lover. Just before he dies, Luzindaro despairs of having lost Medusina and, comparing himself to Macías, as he had done in the beginning of the story, laments ever having fallen in love, and immediately regrets this admission:

> No dexaré de afirmar lo que aquel famoso Macías dixo muy poco antes de su muerte, diciendo al Amor cuán mal pago por tanto tiempo como le había servido le había dado; y murió tan desesperado al fin como yo, viéndome privado del deleite de mi señora, el cual me fué quitado por el sin fe Amor, que quiso que durase tan poco mi gloria, pues para esto mejor me fuera nunca haber amado, ni saber a qué saben sus glorias y dolores, que tanto en mi aposentados están. Mas, ay de mí, qué falsamente he hablado contra mi señora, pues he dicho que valiera más nunca haberla amado. (pp. 105-06)

11 Odell Shepard, *The Lore of the Unicorn* (Boston: Houghton Mifflin, 1930). See in particular Chapter 2, "The Holy Hunt," pp. 41-69. The variations of the association of the unicorn and the virgin can be found on pp. 47-59 and 61-69. Christian allegorizers had managed to relate this virgin-capture to the Incarnation of Christ, but Shepard notes that the recurring association of sexual attraction with the legend is extremely important and can be traced to very early Arabic legends, before finally becoming lost in folklore, with no single source, no single beginning. It is precisely this combination of sexual attraction, death, and the unicorn legend to which Luzindaro alludes.

Taking the remaining ashes of Medusina's burned body, he attempts
to swallow them, is unable to due to his weakened state, and then
dies. Immediately, blackbirds fly through the windows, each carrying
a flame in its beak, and drop them on Luzindaro, who goes up in
flames along with the castle. In place of the castle appears a tomb:

> Y en un punto el castillo y el perfecto amador con todo lo que en él
> había se consumió, de tal arte que más cosa no se vido, más de una
> vega muy llana con un alto padrón de alabastro labrado de muy
> hermosas colores con unos versos...
> AQUI YACE EL SIN VENTURADO AMADOR LUCINDARO (p. 105).

At this point, we are told that, just before he died, Luzindaro sang
these lines, just as Macías had done:

> MENA.
> Vencen el seso sus dulces errores,
> Mas no duran siempre según luego aplacen,
> Pues me hicieron del mal que vos hacen
> Sabed al Amor desamar amadores.
>
> Huid un peligro tan apasionado,
> Sabed ser alegres, dexad de ser tristes,
> Sabed deservir a quien antes servistes,
> A otro que amores dad vuestro cuidado.
>
> Los cuales si diesen por un igual grado
> Sus pocos placeres según su dolor,
> No se quexaría ningun amador,
> Ni desesperararía ningun desamado. (p. 106)[12]

Here, the text has come almost full circle. Earlier in the story,
Luzindaro had ranted against Love's contrary nature and had invoked
that most loyal lover, Macías. Luzindaro hoped that he, too, could
become as legendary a figure as Macías. Macías was his role model
before he attained Medusina and now, after her death, he turns once
again to that role model, but in a different way. The poetry he recites

[12] The poem quoted by Luzindaro near the beginning of the work is the
first half of stanza 106 of *Laberinto de Fortuna* (ed. José Manuel Blecua, Clásicos
Castellanos, 119 [Madrid: Espasa-Calpe, 1943; rpt. 1968]). Luzindaro quotes:
"Amores me dieron corona de amores,/ Porque mi nombre por más bocas
ande./ Entonces no era mi mal menos grande,/Cuando me daban placer sus
dolores," p. 71. The second half of stanza 106 and all of 107 from *Laberinto* are
then quoted by Luzindaro near the end of the work.

is from that section of *Laberinto de Fortuna* (the third sphere, governed by Venus) in which Macías warns against love, instead of celebrating love and loyalty. Since the first half of Mena's stanza had been used in the beginning of *Luzindaro y Medusina* and the rest of the stanza is picked up thirty-five pages later, it is almost as if a *cancionero*-type love poem had been interrupted in order to fill in the details of love's disastrous possibilities.

What follows this is the beginning of a shrine, then followed by a sudden negation of it. It is a sort of reversal of the story of Ardanlier and Liessa in *Estoria de dos amadores*. At the tomb (or, at least, the place where Luzindaro's castle used to be), called here "el padrón," there suddenly appear six beautiful women, whose song is so seductive that it lures many people there. One of the women speaks to the crowd:

> Y la una dellas que más hermosa parecía, puesta en lo más alto de las gradas del padrón, comenzó a dar recias voces a las cuales acudieron gran multitud de gentes, y puestos al derredor, ella en voz alta les comenzó a decir: "Ya, perfectos amadores, habréis visto en que han parado los que en tanto teníades, diciendo que habían gozado de sus dulces amores; y soy aquí enviada de parte de aquel que mandar os puede, para que roguéis al gran Júpiter que haya piedad de sus cuerpos y almas; que pues gozaron en esta vida de sus deleites, gocen en su soberano cielo del que aparejado les estaba por su lealtad. Por tanto, amad firme, y tened fe, sed leales, y no queráis ser tratados según lo fué aquel, que en muriendo todos sus secaces fueron alimentados de sus carnes por la falsedad que con su señora usó. (pp. 106-07)

The other women begin to play their instruments; again, the music is so seductive that, this time, all those who are listening, faint: "Y diciendo esto, sonaron las circo hermosas doncellas sus instrumentos, y con la suavidad que hicieron, cayeron todos en el suelo sin sentido; y a tres voces que la dama tornó a dar, se tornaron a sumir donde jamás parescieron" (p. 107). Nothing remains of the gathering of all the loyal lovers but "el cuerpo afligido" of Luzindaro and the women who attend to it in an unspecified manner. Suddenly, the narrator recalls us to the present by reminding us that we must reject love's false attraction and contemplate the divine, and pursue "aquel que por nosotros en el arbol de la vera cruz se puso por salvarnos" (p. 107).

The ending of the work seems to indicate that even the hoped-for rewards of the loyal lover after death are false hopes: love deceives even after death. Luzindaro had been "un perfecto amador," but, because he despaired at the end of his life, he is left with nothing. This is possibly an answer to Captivo's confident remark in *Processo de cartas*: "Y pues siempre de lealtad no pudo sino bien suceder, quiero guardando sus límites enbiar, antes que me parta, relación de todo lo passado a mi gran amido, Ho. Orz." (p. 88).

Unlike Ardanlier and Liessa, whose love is admired and imitated, and whose tomb became a shrine for lovers and, later, a thriving city, Luzindaro and Medusina enjoy no such popularity. What could have been a shrine, and, indeed, is the site of a gathering of loyal lovers, suddenly disappears and we are left only with the cautionary words of the narrator.

Segura makes no distinction between fact and fiction—he claims, rather, that both *Processo de cartas* and *Luzindaro y Medusina* were translated by him—but he does raise the question of the usefulness of reading "hystorias y libros antiguos" and the value to his contemporaries of the study of "las letras y artes buenas" (p. 31). The ancient philosophers, he asserts, were correct in encouraging the reading of love stories, for example, as a means of moral edification by learning what is best to avoid in this world: "Porque, según Casiodoro, leyendo las hystorias y libros antiguos, alli el prudente halla para ser más prudente y sabio, no haziendo al caso los títulos de las escripturas, porque entre los espinosos cardos se suelen hallar las olorosas rosas y flores" (p. 31).

As mentioned earlier, the notion of fact and fiction, or history and story, arises within the text, for there exists a blurring of the boundaries between author and narrator, between the epistolary section and the story of Luzindaro and Medusina, and even within *Luzindaro y Medusina*. If we were simply to accept Segura's assertion that he translated the works and did not write them, there would be a different problem, one more closely associated with a literary commonplace—the author who denies authorship and declares the work to be discovered by him, and merely copied or translated, as in the case of *Don Quijote*.

Here, the problem is complicated by the identification of Segura with Captivo, the author of the letters in *Processo de cartas*, and the statement by the loyal friend, Ho. Orz., that he sends the Greek work *Luzindaro y Medusina*, which was joined with the present work, as consolation to Captivo: "Os enbío los amores del leal amador Luzindaro y la hermosa Medusina, que con esta obra en el griego juntos estauan, con que creo gran deleyte sentiréys y aliuio muy grande para vuestro mal" (pp. 90-91). The problem for the reader is not so much that we believe Segura when he says he is merely the translator, but whether Segura himself encourages the reader to disbelieve him. Again, as I mentioned earlier, if Segura were adamant about separating himself from the narrative and maintaining his role of mere translator, he would hardly have been so careless as to identify himself with the letter writer in *Processo de cartas* and to suggest that *Luzindaro y Medusina*, ostensibly sent by a friend to Captivo, was joined with the present work, thereby completely destroying the illusion of separate works. Nor would he have included Macías and parts of the fifteenth-century Spanish *Laberinto de Fortuna* is a supposedly Greek work. It is more likely that Segura was playing with the idea of literature and life and the theory of his time, which criticized works which were not true histories as a waste of time, and even harmful to the reader.

It is also possible that Segura played with the blurring of these boundaries as a means of unifying the two disparate parts—the epistolary section and the third-person narrative—and to link these in turn to the prologue, thus requiring the reader to consider the entire work, not just one part, when seeking the lesson to be gained from the reading of it. For example, at the end of *Luzindaro y Medusina*, there is suddenly heard the voice of a narrator who, until now, has not been apparent. The narrator attempts to encourage the reader by expressing the hope that the story of Luzindaro and Medusina will serve both the reader and himself:

> Y a nosotros exemplo para apartarnos de seguir los vanos apetitos del Amor... Y con entera voluntad humildemente le supliquemos quiera esta pequeña fructa sacada de mi pobre ingenio, y sea para exemplo, y no en perjuicio, de las que la leyeren, para que se aparten de tal pestilencia, como es Amor ponzoñoso, y les dé gracia para que vayan a gozar de su soberana gloria. (p. 107)

This statement of the hope for our edification returns us to the prologue, where Segura mentions not only that there are lessons to be learned from reading what follows the prologue, but that the lesson refers to love as something "ponçoñoso";

> Los lectores leyéndole [the work] más a la clara veran de qué arte deste ponçoñoso fuego de amor se an de guardar: viendo y leyendo en él muchas cosas antiguas en las quales están esculpidas todas las ponçonas del mundo de que nos hemos de evitar siguiendo el estudio de las letras y otros nobles exercicios de que vuestra merced tan abastado está. (p. 31)

Thus, Segura is able to present two kinds of narrative, one in first person and one in third person, but he also manages to link them subtly, by means of themes, imagery and a certain confusion of narrative voice, in order to require the reader to consider both parts in his interpretation of the story. That *Luzindaro y Medusina* has normally been eliminated from critical concern indicates that Segura was perhaps less successful than he would have liked, but it seems quite clear that it was his intention, at least, that we consider *Processo de cartas* and *Luzindaro y Medusina* to be two halves of a whole.

### Juan de Segura's Possible Debt to Rodríguez del Padrón: Return to the Prototype

Juan de Segura's *Processo de cartas de amores*, in its entirety, continues the dialectic of literature and life that is found in the other sentimental romances of violent love. Structurally, it is most like Rodríguez del Padrón's *Siervo libre de amor*, the earliest sentimental romance: both are bipartite narratives, although *Siervo libre de amor* consists of an autobiographical frame story and an intercalated narrative in third person, while Segura's *Processo de cartas de amores* consists of two distinct parts, easily separated.[13] Both *Siervo's* frame story and Segura's epistolary section tell the story of unnamed lovers—Siervo, Captivo and Servidora—while the third-person narratives are detailed stories of named lovers in named geographical settings. The frame story and *Processo de cartas* are stories of frustrated love, the other two tales of fulfilled, yet ultimately violent, love. And, just as Siervo learned a lesson from the intercalated tale, so, too, Captivo can take consolation and learn from the tragedy of *Luzindaro y Medusina*. Siervo and Captivo, both brokenhearted over their unsuccessful or frustrated affairs, learn about the violent nature of love and that they are better off without earthly love.

Thematically then, as well as structurally, the stories are strikingly similar. Siervo finds that he can go on in life, without another love, because he has been loyal and loyalty has been portrayed as the greatest virtue. But it does seem that, in the future, he will shun earthly love for the love of God. Captivo, too, is encouraged to accept

---

[13] Durán, in *Estructura y técnicas*, refers to a similarity between *Siervo libre de amor* and *Processo de cartas de amores*, but does no more than mention it: "La novelita que la 'manda' al autor un amigo, para que le sirva de consuelo, *Quexa y aviso contra el amor, Luzindaro y Medusina* sigue la línea trazada por Juan Rodríguez del Padrón en la *Estoria de dos amadores*," p. 46.

and cherish the love he did experience, but to beware love's further entrapment. He, too, will turn to God. The subsequent rejection of earthly love does not automatically imply that those who did follow the call of earthly love were wrong in any moral sense. For example, both Luzindaro and Ardanlier commit suicide, one from despair, the other by the sword. But the moral question of suicide plays no role in Captivo's judgment of Luzindaro, just as it does not in the case of Siervo and his judgment of Ardanlier. We know this because both protagonists in the cautionary tales are treated as victims, as sympathetic figures, and not as sinners or enemies of society. Moreover, the Catholic mores of Segura's time cannot be applied *ipso facto* to the story of Luzindaro and Medusina: hence, the mask of the Greek story translated into Castilian, a mask which neatly avoids this very question of the morality of suicide and the Catholic belief of the subsequent certainty of eternal hell as punishment for this sin. In other words, Luzindaro is not faulted for having committed the unforgivable sin of suicide; the question simply does not arise. Rather, the very nature of love is questioned and shown to lead to disorder and to disintegrate into violence as its end. Learning from these examples, without experiencing the potential violence themselves, Captivo and Siervo both renounce earthly love for something much more certain, with the promise of being everlasting.

A further link between the works is the presence of Macías in the interpolated *Estoria de dos amadores*, and the poetry which follows it, and in *Luzindaro y Medusina*. Apart from representing the theme of loyalty, Macías can be seen as warning future lovers; in *Laberinto* and, by consequence, *Luzindaro y Medusina*, Macías says: "Sabed al Amor desamar amadores" and "A otro que amores dad vuestro cuidado." As we recall, Rodríguez del Padrón's first-person narrator initially divides *Siervo libre de amor* into three parts, the second and third of which are "el tiempo que bien amó y fue desamado" and "el tiempo que no amó ni fue amado" (p. 66). In one of the final stanzas of the poem "Aunque me vedes asý,/catyvo, libre naçý," (presumably part of "el tiempo que no amó ni fue amado,") one stanza refers to Macías:

> No se que postremería
> ayan buena los mis días,
> quando el gentil Maçías
> priso muerte por tal vía. (pp. 109-10)

The example of Macías as ill-fated lover, then, appears in *Siervo libre de amor*, although indirectly in the poetry, and is in accord with his portrayal in *Luzindaro y Medusina*. As mentioned in the first chapter of this study, Rodríguez del Padrón enjoyed associating himself with Macías, the legend, and was, moreover, associated later with Juan de Mena, so they appear to be a somewhat natural trio in *Luzindaro y Medusina*.[14]

The major difference between Rodríguez del Padrón's treatment of earthly love and Segura's treatment is one of degree. Siervo awakens to a realization of a higher love, while maintaining his belief in the power of loyalty. Segura, on the other hand, demonstrates that the courtly ideal of loyalty, while not wrong in itself, merely results in one more disillusionment. Perhaps it is not accidental that, in Segura's work, instead of the enchanted tomb/shrine of Rodriguez del Padrón's lovers, we find "una vega muy llana con un alto padron" (p. 105). The word "padron" appears in Rodríguez del Padrón's work, also, to describe the location of the enchanted tomb: "E llegando apres dela rroca en que era fyrmado y sotyl mente obrado el secreto palaçio, que oy dia llaman la rroca del padron, he aqui Yrena, acompañada de dueñas y donzellas, vestidas de su escura librea" (p. 69). It is possible that Segura uses both this reference and the author's name, as a means of demythifying the earlier example, in a scene which reverses Rodríguez del Padrón's idea of order restored in order to emphasize love as a force of disorder.

Thus, with Segura's work the Spanish sentimental romance of violent love is shown to come full circle, both thematically and structurally. *Processo de cartas de amores* appears to rely strongly on the format and theme of the prototype, *Siervo libre de amor*, while on the other hand, it is shown to extend itself generically, through Segura's distinction of having written the first completely epistolary work.

---

[14] I have been unable to find evidence which would prove that Segura definitely knew *Siervo libre de amor*. There is no reference to the author or his work in the text other than my hypothesis that "padrón" in Segura's work refers to Rodríguez del Padrón and his work. We do not know anything about the life of Juan de Segura, so it is impossible to prove anything through a knowledge of his biography. What can be documented, however, is the sixteenth century's familiarity with Rodríguez del Padrón and the lovers Ardanlier and Liessa. Moreover, he was associated with both Macías and Juan de Mena. For a discussion of Juan Rodríguez' popularity, see Chapter 4, "Fama e Influencia," pp. 83-88 of César Hernández Alonso's *"Siervo libre de amor" de Juan Rodríguez del Padrón* (Valladolid: Universidad, 1970) and Maria Rosa Lida de Malkiel, "Juan Rodríguez del Padrón: Influencia," *NRFH*, 8 (1954), 1-38.

# 6

# Toward an Approach to the
# Spanish Sentimental Romances

"El amor está en las carnes desgarradas por la sed,
en la choza diminuta que lucha con la inundación;
el amor está en los fasos donde luchan las sierpes del hambre,
en el triste mar que mece los cadáveres de las gaviotas
y en el oscurísímo beso punzante debajo de las almohadas."
FEDERICO GARCÍA LORCA, *Poeta en Nueva York*

## Introduction: Desire and Death

N THE INTRODUCTION to this study, I suggested
that some connection might be found between
these romances which would elucidate their
generic unity. There are superficial features
which caused critics to connect them even while
expressing reservations about doing so. The
works themselves seemed to defy categorization, no doubt for the obvious reason that they
are so very different even though they employ many of the same
elements.

The first step in my own approach was to divide those works
which I termed romances of violent love from those of frustrated
love. This seemed to be an important point: after all, the lamentations
of rejected lovers hardly compare in magnitude and gravity with
actual evidence of violence and death. The decision to discuss exclu-
sively the works of violent love is based on more than an arbitrary—
albeit ultimately fortunate for this study—division of the sentimental
genre. Desire and death, or more broadly love and death, are bound in
a manner which has fascinated mankind for centuries.

Elizabeth Sewell, in her elaboration of different aspects of the human condition, convincingly argues the connection of love and death, including in her commentary poetic, philosophical, and psychological evidence. She says:

> This last figure of the poets that we shall look at, love and death, or, as I prefer to write it here, love-and-death, is not merely a figure in poetic method or a matter of literature...Love and death, separately, seem obvious enough subjects for poets; at least, a great deal of poetry has been written on or around them. But for the rest of us? And why the hyphening, the linking of them into love-and-death which may seem to us strange or even morbid? Yet what seems to us strange in cold print is in another context so familiar in our day-to-day lives that we scarcely even notice it any more. The merest glance at the world of popular culture in which we are all willy-nilly submerged discloses the degree to which all of us and particularly the young are obsessed by images of love and death in the elementary form of sex and violence, not separated but in some secretive yet blatant embrace...Distorted form of love-and-death though sex-and-violence may be, they provide evidence of the connection, and of this pair as in some way essential to us beyond the solely physical.[1]

To suppose that the medieval poets seized upon the connection of love and death is not unfounded. As the two great topics of poetry—unsolvable mysteries both—it is no surprise that they should appear with great frequency in literature. The surprise comes when they occur in a recognizably causal relationship, especially in medieval works, since misfortune in love was usually attributed to the beloved's coldness or fickleness, the intervention of another person, God's will or Fortune's inconstancy, and not to desire or to love itself.[2] It seems quite clear, however, that to some writers of the fifteenth and sixteenth centuries, human passionate desires alone were enough to engender violence.

Desire was a popular topic with medieval man and, as Evelyn Birge Vitz says, it is behind most of the narratives of the Middle

---

[1] *The Human Metaphor* (Notre Dame: University Press, 1964), pp. 156-57. For the explanations of the connections of love and death and some poetic analyses, see Chapter 5, "The Figure of Love and Death," pp. 156-98.

[2] This is not to imply that there is any unintentional causality in these works, which is mainly a modern notion. Desire is the motivating force and, as in the case of *Grisel y Mirabella*, can seem to take on its own momentum, but it is clear that the violence can be traced to human desire even if the characters themselves fail to recognize this.

Ages.[3] Some of her observations are most pertinent to my own arguments. She discusses the provocation to action in medieval texts, ascertains it to be human desires (here, she uses desire in its broad sense of human wants, not confining it to love) and shows how the text proceeds to fulfill or not fulfill those needs. It is her conclusion—that the poets show man's desire to be largely inefficient in bringing about the desired result—that is most enlightening. In addition, desire is shown to misinform the recipient of what he actually requires and how he should go about attaining it.[4] The protagonists pursue love, for example, in the form of the beloved as the ultimate goal, which is precisely what brings about their downfall.

In the Spanish sentimental romances of violent love, we find more than a passing connection between love and death. The individual analyses in this study served to underscore the uniqueness of these particular literary situations of love and ultimate death. However, there are other features to indicate that this connection goes beyond the obvious plot to be embedded in numerous ways in these works.

Alone, these examples are inconclusive and may seem insignificant but, together, and especially when we keep in mind the work as a whole, they bespeak the presence—consciously or subconsciously included by the author—of the link of love and death. Consider, for one, the place where love is born in San Pedro's *Arnalte y Lucenda*: Arnalte is instantly smitten with Lucenda when he sees her at her father's funeral, normally not an occasion to have love on one's mind. But Sewell says:

> At the social and organizational level of humanity they appear once again in conection. Historians derive man's earliest temporary settlements from these two, in their more institutional forms of marriage and begetting and of burial; and from this the whole development of city and state and all their institutions may follow. (p. 158)

[3] See "Desire and Causality in Medieval Narrative," *RR*, 71 (1980), 213-43 in which she says: "The medieval *récit*—as many readers and critics have noted—is filled with passionate desires, of ardent appetites of all sorts and for all sorts of things. These desires, these appetites provide not only different kinds of content but different kinds of structure as well for the works in which they occur," p. 213.

[4] She states: "Desire is presented as a narrative motor, in the sense that it initiates the action, sets off the causal chain, in the narrative.... But if desire begins the chain of events, human agency (motored by desire) is not represented as competent, of itself, to achieve its ends. Human desire has energy but not great efficiency," p. 242.

While the case of *Arnalte y Lucenda* does not extend itself to the development of city and state, this is certainly so in *Estoria de dos amadores* in which the lovers' tomb becomes the center of a city.

In Juan de Flores' *Grisel y Mirabella*, when Mirabella has been condemned to death and the people of the kingdom parade to the site of the expected execution, there is a general lament among them that they had expected to gather together for the wedding of their princess, not for her funeral:

> Y depues que el dia fue llegado que Mirabella moriesse: quien podria scriuir las cosas de gran magnificencia que para su muerte stauan ordenadas. y todas muy conformes a tristexa segund que el caso lo requeria. ansi fiestas tan tristes: como el dia de sus bodas se le pensauan fazer alegres. (p. 358)

The idea of death and rebirth is another area of consideration. It is a constant in romance, according to Frye, but is particularly important for us when it is consistently linked with love.[5] Sewell gives us a literary example of this from Shakespeare's *All's Well That Ends Well* in which Helena, outlining her concept of the perfect lover, includes among his attributes that he be a phoenix. Sewell's explanation for this stems in part from the belief that, "at the physical level, sex and death have been felt for a very long time to possess a formal symmetry of dynamic the one to the other" (p. 158). The phoenix, we recall, appears in Segura's *Luzindaro y Medusina*. After Luzindaro and Medusina's wedding, Actelasia the prophetess-sorceress predicts the death of the lovers:

> Cuando la blanca paloma perdiere su ser, entonces la gran Fénix comenzará a alimentarse de su ceniza, hasta que tenga compañía a la blanca paloma que aguardándole estará. Y porque esto vendrá como tengo dicho, no penséis que las cosas en un ser de contino puedan permanescer. (p. 94)

There are other examples of different types. San Pedro's attach-

---

[5] Northrop Frye, *The Secular Scripture: A Study of the Structure of Romance* (Cambridge, MA: Harvard University Press, 1976; rpt. 1978). The theme of death and rebirth, especially in the form of lost and regained self-identity, is to be found throughout romance and throughout Frye's discussion of it. One reason for this, he says, is that: "One of the most fundamental human realizations is that passing from death to rebirth is impossible for the same individual; hence the theme of substitution for death runs all through literature, religion, and ritual," p. 89.

ment of a poem, "Las angustias de Santa Maria," to the prose narrative *Arnalte y Lucenda* has been criticized. It was suggested in an earlier chapter that the Eve/Mary dichotomy may, to a certain extent, justify this poetic addition. Possibly, since the entire poem revolves around speculation on Mary's emotions on losing her son, we can see again the connection of love and death. This illustration of love and death, unlike *Arnalte* proper, shows a positive aspect of the death which comes from love, in man's redemption from sin. It serves as a contrast to the love story which precedes it, in which love results in death and exile.

The connection of love and death suggests itself in both *Grisel y Mirabella* and *Cárcel de Amor* where the penalty for sexual transgressions is death. Here, society has chosen this path, these laws, and creates a connection between sex and death and, in doing so, reinforces the natural association which man, perhaps subconsciously, already knows to exist.

Finally, the particular literature at hand lends itself to the exploration of the question of violence and death simply because its foundation and impetus, the courtly love lyric, consists of a vocabulary of sexual euphemisms, often paradoxical, whose examples are words of violence, of dying, of destruction.[6] When the authors of the sentimental romances attempt to play out these poetic paradoxes in prose, violence is the narrative result.

The main difference between the first story considered in this study, *Estoria de dos amadores*, and the others is that Rodríguez del

---

[6] Keith Whinnom, "Hacia una interpretación y apreciación de las canciones del *Cancionero general* de 1511," *Filología*, 13 (1968-69), 361-81. See also his *La poesía amatoria de la época de los Reyes Católicos*, Durham Modern Language Series, Hispanic Monographs, 2 (Durham: University, 1981), especially Chapter III, "El problema del lenguaje," pp. 34-46. Words of violence by no means cover the extensive vocabulary of sexual euphemisms within *cancionero* poetry. The point of contact between the courtly love lyric and the cancionero poetry is that when words of violence are employed, they often appear in paradoxical phrases which, in the poetry, lead to an impasse, while in the romances they lead to inevitably violent actions. This vocabulary is not confined to Spanish examples, or even those of the Provençal poets. Elizabeth Sewell tells us: "In the English language the connection between love and death became so close as to permit linguistic identity by the seventeenth century—possibly earlier for all I know. Certainly in Dryden's poetry the verb 'to die' is in familiar use as an expression for female sexual orgasm. Freud comments on 'the likeness of the condition that follows complete sexual satisfaction to dying' in Chapter IV of *The Ego and the Id*, 1923," p. 158.

Padrón tries to show that, in spite of the resultant deaths, life can spawn from love after all, whereas this is not the case in any of the other works under consideration. That a thriving port city rises whose center and genesis is the lovers' tomb, is a tribute to the love portrayed in the work. Also, *Estoria de dos amadores* is the only romance which points without question to a particular human being—Ardanlier's father—as the culprit, the reason why the lovers perished. Rodríguez del Padrón points out that love will triumph and the result will in some way be positive. The other romances sadly demonstrate that love—as desire and passion—also will triumph but the result is negative. In the former, love triumphs with, or for, the lovers; in the latter, it is a triumph over the lovers.

This chapter deals with the structural devices which link all the romances of violent love. Within this group—the romances of violent love—can be found two distinct types. The first group explores love in more general terms, through its effect on society, while the other underscores the deleterious nature of love, but goes on to provide a solution for mankind.

*Literature and Life in the Spanish Sentimental Romances: Structural Considerations*

The Spanish sentimental romances, in their broadest considerations, are prose amplifications of the situations presented or alluded to in courtly love lyric. The concept of examining a primarily literary code in the context of real-life situations was not the invention of these authors. That reality and the emotions expressed in courtly literature—specifically the love-lyric—were not exact copies was the realization of at least one poet: the anonymous author of the thirteenth-century Provenzal work, *Flamenca*. Recent studies of *Flamenca* illuminate its essentially satirical nature, a change from earlier times when critics more often took this literature at face value and assumed it to exemplify definite rules of courtly love.[7]

Suzanne Fleischman's "Dialectic Structures in *Flamenca*" is an examination of the opposing forces of individual desire and social convention, a dialectic which, I believe, functions in the Spanish works as well.[8] She says, "The *Flamenca* poet attempts what the lyric

---

[7] See, for example, C. S. Lewis, *The Allegory of Love: A Study in Medieval Tradition* (Oxford: Clarendon Press, 1936; rpt. 1977) and A. J. Denomy, *The Heresy of Courtly Love* (New York: MacMullen, 1947; rpt. Gloucester, MA: Peter Smith, 1965).

[8] *RF*, 92 (1980), 223-46.

poets could not, given the inherent constraints of their genre: he tests the viability of these ideals by placing them in contact with what purports to be 'real life'" (p. 224). The Spanish authors make the same attempt, in varying degrees and with varying success, and their methods are the following: 1) They incorporate the love lyric—a literary vehicle—into the "real" lives of their characters in an attempt to recreate the dialectic of literature and life which existed in fifteenth-century Spain. What was primarily a literary code—courtly love and its ensuing poetry—was being accepted and promoted as desirable, necessary and real behavior.[9] In general this poetry represents the artificial, the contrived, the literary, not any provable or desirable reality. The insertion of poetry into the prose served to juxtapose the code which existed in the speaker's/character's background, external to the text, with the purported history being related. For example, Grimalte, when he switches from dialogue to poetry, employs recognizable turns of phrase from courtly poetry. That the real author of Grimalte's poetry was Alonso de Córdoba, a *cancionero* poet, should not deter us from examining the consequences of the juxtaposition of this poetry within the prose because, as it stands, it is to be taken by the readers entirely as Grimalte's story—dialogue, narration and poetry—so the question of who actually wrote the poetry should not concern us here as much as the fact that the poetry is incorporated into the text as if it were part of everyday speech. This work does not intend to show us how Grimalte came to discover the courtly code or exactly what constitutes the code, but to show how these ideals function and influence a real life, contained in this "true" history of Grimalte's trials and tribulations. 2) To further the illusion of literature and life, each of the works somehow incorporates or juxtaposes first and third-person narration, sometimes implying that the third-person narrative is story while the other is history as in *Processo de cartas de amores y Quexa y aviso contra el Amor.* Each of the works somehow implies real life versus fictional life or blurs the lines between them in order to confuse us, but also remind us of the dual and occasionally indistinguishable duty of words to record both truth and fiction. 3) The third common method is that each author in some way sets off physical love from frustrated love. Even though each author uses this method differently and in varying degrees, every

---

[9] Roger Boase, *The Troubadour Revival: A Study of Social Change and Traditionalism in Late Medieval Spain* (London: Routledge and Kegan Paul, 1978), documents the imitation of courtly literature as a real phenomenon in fifteenth-century Spain.

work either has two sets of lovers, one pair whose relationship is physical, the other not, or has a triangular relationship.

In general this dialectic serves to show that when human passions are unfettered, as they usually are, given human nature, the result is a violent encounter of some kind. For the most part, when the courtly code is followed and the lovers only exchange letters and no physical union is attained, no violence is unleashed, merely frustration and lamentations. The following diagrams help to illustrate the structure of the romances and the various ways in which they employ the above-mentioned categories.

1. *Siervo libre de amor* and *Estoria de dos amadores*

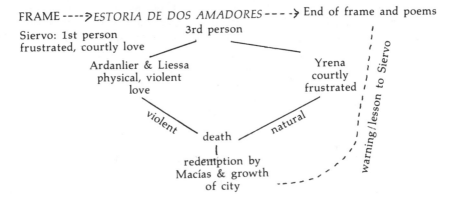

One of Rodríguez del Padrón's goals was to relate his own failed attempt at a courtly love affair. Using this autobiographical story as the frame, he proceeded to include as the structural and thematic nucleus of his narrative the tale of Ardanlier, Liessa and Yrena, a story of physical love and frustrated love and the creation of a shrine and, later, a city with the tomb of the lovers as its inspiration. My analysis focused on how Rodríguez del Padrón showed the manner in which another's story could serve as an *exemplum* and resolution to one's own dilemma, a not uncommon technique as Rolfs demonstrated.[10] Even though Ardanlier and Liessa die violent deaths and

[10] Daniel J. Rolfs, "Dante, Petrarch, Boccaccio and the Problem of Suicide," *RR*, 67 (1976), 200-25. As mentioned in Chapter I, non-Christian works or the characters within them could serve as moral *exempla*, either positive or negative, without the issue of church doctrine being taken into account. In other words, suicide, which is a mortal sin according to the church, did not necessarily imply a judgment against these characters in other works.

Yrena's reward for her unwavering devotion to Ardanlier's memory seems slight, those same acts of loyalty redeem the lovers and make their lives and deaths purposeful. In the same way Siervo, of the frame story, realizes that in spite of the dissolution of his own love affair, his loyalty to the beloved never wavered, and this liberates him from feelings of guilt and failure.

In the frame story there is only the lover, the beloved, and the friend. No physical action is described—all seems to be conducted along the approved guidelines of courtly affairs. The friend who reveals to the beloved that Siervo has confided in him about the affair, thus breaking the rule of strict secrecy, is perhaps the seed of the jealous rival so prominent in San Pedro's two romances. At the broadest level, the frame story shows a love triangle, although we do not really know if the false friend is interested in Siervo's beloved for himself. It is, nonetheless, a story of false friendship, of loyalty betrayed. The opposite occurs in *Estoria de dos amadores*: Yrena loves Ardanlier with all her heart but pushes aside her own feelings when Ardanlier declares that his own true love will always be Liessa.

We see, then, that the entire narrative is an obviously bipartite one composed of structural and thematic contrasts and comparisons.

## 2. *Triste deleytaçión*

The introduction here of a text not included in the previous chapters would seem to be an unnecessary digression, but the unusual case of *Triste deleytaçión* deserves mention. An anonymous fifteenth-century romance, it existed until recently solely in a codex belonging to the Biblioteca de Catalunya in Barcelona. Until E. Michael Gerli and Regula Rohland de Langbehn's recent editions, *Triste deleytaçión* was known only through Martín de Riquer's article in which he discussed possible authors, provided some selections from the manuscript and speculated in general about the date of composition and geographical location of the story.[11] There is no evidence to prove that *Triste deleytaçión* was known outside of Catalonia (and therefore accessible to writers such as Flores and San Pedro), but it is an

---

[11] *Triste deleytaçión: An Anonymous Fifteenth Century Castilian Romance*, ed. E. Michael Gerli (Washington: Georgetown University Press, 1983; *Triste deleytaçión*, ed. Regula Rohland de Langbehn (Madrid: Fundación Universitaria Española, 1984); Martín de Riquer, "*Triste deleytaçión*, novela castellana del siglo XV," *RFE*, 40 (1956), 33-65.

interesting link in terms of the evolution of the structure of the Castilian romances.

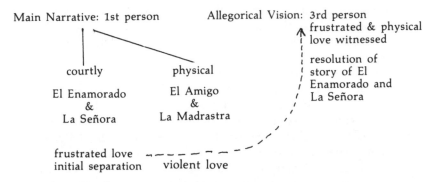

Main Narrative: 1st person          Allegorical Vision: 3rd person
                                    frustrated & physical
                                    love witnessed

                                    resolution of
          courtly        physical   story of El
                                    Enamorado and
     El Enamorado      El Amigo      La Señora
          &               &
     La Señora      La Madrastra

frustrated love
initial separation    violent love

*Triste deleytaçión* fits chronologically between *Siervo libre de amor* and *Tractado de amores de Arnalte y Lucenda* and exhibits features of binarism and doubling. It is clearly divided in two parts, an autobiographical one (which abruptly switches to third person) and, after the initial separation of the lovers, a second part, an allegorical vision witnessed by the male protagonist, El Enamorado.

The characters are compared: the lovers El Enamorado and la Señora, whose encounters stop just short of comsummation, meet no worse fates than separation and frustration. The other pair of lovers, El Amigo and La Madrastra (married to La Señora's father) carry on an adulterous love affair. The unsurprising conclusion to that affair is the murder of La Madrastra by her husband's henchmen. In these romances women tend to pay with their lives for sexual transgressions.

The first part of *Triste deleytaçión* is fairly realistic (within the conventions of medieval literature, that is). The second part—the vision of lovers in paradise, purgatory and hell, obviously of Dantesque influence—is full of literary and historical lovers.[12] Although we do not know anything about the author of *Triste deleytaçión*, we do know that he was familiar with the name Rodríguez del Padrón: this author appears in the list of literary and historical figures.[13] Within

[12] Gerli discusses the Italian influence in the introduction to his edition of *Triste deleytaçión*, pp. vii-xxv. Marina Scordilis Brownlee studies the relationship between Boccaccio's *Decameron* and *Triste deleytaçión* in her forthcoming "Structures of Authority in *Triste deleytaçión*."

[13] Gerli, *Triste deleytaçión*, p. 121, "Rodrigo del Pedrón" and p. 11, "Lisa y Ardanlier, fijo del Rey Creos de Mondoya.

this allegorical part we are treated to vignettes of lovers, and even witness a story of violent love and hear one of frustrated love. Two women are being chased: one is killed by her pursuer, the other, saved by El Enamorado, tells of her unhappy affair and how her lover killed himself in despair.

3. *Tractado de amores de Arnalte y Lucenda*

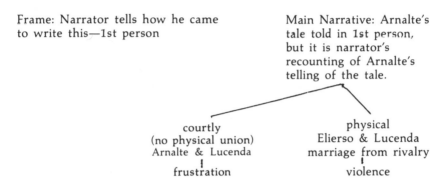

Frame: Narrator tells how he came to write this—1st person

Main Narrative: Arnalte's tale told in 1st person, but it is narrator's recounting of Arnalte's telling of the tale.

courtly
(no physical union)
Arnalte & Lucenda
↕
frustration

physical
Elierso & Lucenda
marriage from rivalry
↕
violence

In *Arnalte y Lucenda* physical and courtly relationships are contrasted and compared in two ways. First, Arnalte recites courtly love-lyric in the expected manner, but this contrasts with his overt pursuit of Lucenda, and is not part of the courtly code. This exemplifies the paradoxical nature of Arnalte's actions and, moreover, can be seen as emblematic of the quandary of distinguishing literature from life. He wants to follow the literary code in his daily life, but it imposes restrictions on the emotions which he, as the archetypal ardent lover, cannot withstand.

The second example of the clash between physical and courtly love is in the development of the love triangle of Arnalte, Lucenda and Elierso. Love is shown to inspire jealousy, which, in turn, engenders violence. Literature and life are more subtly compared and merged in *Arnalte y Lucenda* than in other romances, which makes it perhaps the most realistic of the sentimental romances.

The narrator recounts Arnalte's recounting of the tale, so we have a sense of an on-going text: we are brought from Arnalte's exile, through the tale of how he arrived there, and back to the present when Arnalte asks our narrator to spread his story, which, of course, the narrator does.

4. *Cárcel de Amor*

1st person: Narrator takes active part & relates tale

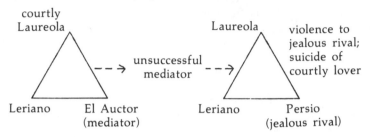

As he does in *Arnalte y Lucenda*, San Pedro here displays the negative power of jealousy within a love triangle. Literature and life merge in the narrative as it progresses from allegory to a more realistic situation. In the opening pages, desire is a Wild Man, who has captured the lovesick Leriano. There is a description of the Wild Man and his habitation, the prison of love. El Auctor, the narrator, acts as messenger between the prisoner, Leriano, and the object of his affections, Laureola. Once Laureola writes back to Leriano, hope is inspired, and the allegorical prison disappears and is replaced by real characters in a fairly believable situation.

Desire is not a hairy man one can see and outwit or conquer: it is a powerful force of unsuspected dimensions. Leriano, smitten with Laureola, thinks only of his love for her. His jealous rival, also captured by the power of desire, wishes Leriano and Laureola harm: Persio would rather see them dead than permit their love to continue. His jealousy causes him to invent more in their relationship than had existed, and we know that his own death occurs as a result of all these inventions. One can readily disbelieve the existence of a Wild Man, especially as a warning against love, but the actions provoked by Desire—a real Wild Man or not—are frightening and believable. Here, death comes as the end merely from the suggestion of a physical relationship which transgressed society's rules.

In addition to the reality of desire, literature and life are brought to mind again by the transition of the narrator from observer and teller of the tale to active participant in the story. The power of the written word is underscored by the fact that the narrator records the experience and does not rely on the verbal retelling of it. He realizes his failure as the mediator in the love triangle and wishes to use this tale as a warning.

5. *Grisel y Mirabella*

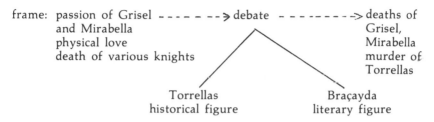

3rd person narrative with 1st person debate taking
almost 3/4 of the textual space

frame: passion of Grisel - - - - - --> debate - - - - - - - -> deaths of
and Mirabella                                                                    Grisel,
physical love                                                                    Mirabella
death of various knights                                                    murder of
Torrellas

Torrellas                                    Braçayda
historical figure                        literary figure

No poetry appears in *Grisel y Mirabella*. In that case, any sense of
the conflation of literature and life, or the relationship of what goes
on in *Grisel y Mirabella*, a literary text, to the reality of fifteenth-
century Spain, must come from some other narrative technique.
Flores does not officially separate his narrative into first and third-
person but he is able, nevertheless, to play with the idea of story and
history. *Grisel y Mirabella* gains a sense of reality, or at least, a
confusion of literature and life, when Torrellas, a real-life fifteenth-
century Catalan, arrives in Scotland for the great debate over the
vices and virtues of men and women. His verbal sparring partner and
later his lust-interest (to call her a love interest would be incorrect) is
a literary character come to life—Braçayda of the *Crónica troyana*. That
a historical figure should pair up with a literary one is a clever move.
To further enhance the truth/fiction dichotomy, the main role of
Braçayda and Torrellas is as debaters. As a dialogue, the debate would
be more realistic than the kind of third-person narration found in
these romances. Also, this debate leaves behind the particulars of the
case of Grisel and Mirabella and argues existential questions about
men and women and their true nature. Were this section to be
removed from the text, it could easily be read as a separate entity.

6. *Grimalte y Gradissa*

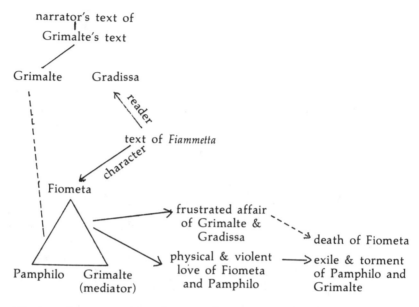

Flores achieves in *Grimalte y Gradissa* a triumph of literary games-manship. The reader's task of sorting the literary from the real is an impossible one. Unlike the authors of some works in which the confusion may be the consequence of sloppy writing, Flores presents a calculated confusion.

As the diagram illustrates, there are various texts within the work. It is difficult to know at what point Grimalte thinks of the opinions and comments that he records, since he is retelling what he wrote at the time of the experience. All the characters recite poetry, although Grimalte and Fiometa do so with far more frequency than do the other two main characters. Gradissa is a reader of the auto-biography of which another character, Fiometa, is the author.

As for the contrast of physical love and courtly love, Flores defines the two relationships (Pamphilo/Fiometa and Grimalte/Gradissa) along these very lines. Pamphilo and Fiometa shared a passionate, adulterous relationship before the beginning of the text of *Grimalte y Gradissa*. It was their break-up which caused Fiometa to write down her bitter experience. Grimalte and Gradissa's relationship was con-ducted along courtly lines. Here, literature serves as an *exemplum* to the wary Gradissa. The continuance of her relationship with Grimalte becomes contingent upon Grimalte's successful completion of a mission: to bring Pamphilo and Fiometa together once again. Since Grimalte feels that Pamphilo behaves shamefully towards Fiometa, he takes on the role of her defender, a role which can cause him to be the third point of a triangle, as the mediator between Pamphilo and Fiometa. He imitates Pamphilo and, in so doing, shares in the pain which is usually reserved for those characters in romances of violent love who have indulged in passionate affairs. The courtly relationship of Grimalte and Gradissa ends in frustration, while the relationship of Fiometa and Pamphilo ends in death for one and exile and torment for the other. But Grimalte willingly shares this physical and mental anguish with Pamphilo, leaving Gradissa the only character to have benefited from having read about someone else's misfortune.

7. *Processo de cartas de amores y Quexa y aviso contra el Amor*

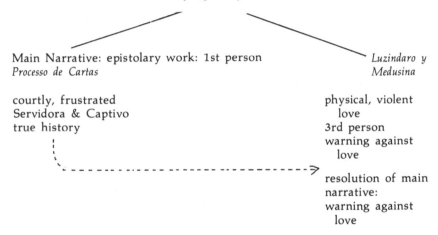

Main Narrative: epistolary work: 1st person
*Processo de Cartas*

*Luzindaro y Medusina*

courtly, frustrated
Servidora & Captivo
true history

physical, violent
love
3rd person
warning against
love

resolution of main
narrative:
warning against
love

As in *Siervo libre de amor* in which the third-person narrative gives consolation to the bereaved Siervo, so too does the third-person narrative *Luzindaro y Medusina* purport to console by analogy and warn by outright advice the unhappy Captivo of the epistolary part of the work.

Captivo and Servidora are spared the ultimate and inevitable grief of a love relationship by the forceful intervention of Servidora's brothers, who quickly put a stop to the exchange of letters and deposit her in a convent. It is truly an example, as explained by Rolfs, of tragedy realized and tragedy averted.[14] The textual multiplicity exists in spite of the tendency of publishers or editors to eliminate consideration of the appended tale *Luzindaro y Medusina*, because it is clearly the author's intention that both parts be regarded as one. In addition, there is more confusion because the author disclaims having written the second part, saying instead that it was sent by a friend who translated it from the Greek. Even though there is some confusion as to the author of each part, the romance is more like *Siervo libre de amor* than any of the others (except perhaps *Triste deleytaçión*) in its simplicity of structure, with its clearly defined bipartite narrative.

To help draw some conclusions about the sentimental romances, let us turn to the question of generic unity. In "Spatial Form in Medieval Romance", Norris J. Lacy reminds us that the relationship of scenes in romance is often not by sequence or causality, but by analogy. Citing Vinaver's pioneer study of romance, Lacy reaffirms the need to remember the inapplicability of a term such as "organic unity" and to consider instead "generic unity."[15] Good medieval works, Lacy continues, express their own peculiar brand of unity in that the various episodes, through their use of imagery, form, or theme, are appropriate, rather than absolutely indispensable to the story: "The unity of the work derives from the fact that in some sense the episodes are of the *same kind*, hence *generic unity*" (p. 169). Although my previous analyses have shown how the sentimental romances differ, they have in addition indicated certain similarities of theme. These similarities extend to structural ones, as we saw in the diagrams, which can be called binarism, doubling, and textual multiplicity.

William Ryding explains that the predominant structural edifice of medieval works was the bipartite narrative.[16] Binarism can refer to anything from the prevalence of dual characters, opposing moralities, a definite sense of good and evil, to the bipartite narrative. For the

[14] In "Dante, Petrarch...," Rolfs explains that very often a bipartite narrative will have the inner tale as the disaster or tragedy realized while the outer narrative or frame will represent tragedy averted.

[15] Lacy's article appears in *YFS*, 51 (1974), 160-69. He bases his own arguments on two studies by Eugène Vinaver: *The Rise of Romance* (Oxford: Clarendon Press, 1971) and *Form and Meaning in Medieval Romance* ([London]: Modern Humanities Research Association, 1966).

[16] William W. Ryding, *Structure in Medieval Narrative* (The Hague: Mouton, 1971). See also Tony Hunt, "The Structure of Medieval Narrative," *JES*, 3 (1973), 295-328.

kind of structural complexity existing in these sentimental romances, the term binarism alone is not enough to do it justice—hence, the inclusion of the word doubling.

Doubles and doubling prevail in romance,[17] and are not uncommon features in other literature. What is important to remember, especially since the degree and type of doubling vary greatly in the Spanish sentimental romances, is that doubling can refer to exact duplication but does not necessarily do so. Robert Rogers, in *A Psychoanalytic Study of the Double in Literature*, tells us that the term "doubling" is a convenient catch-all phrase which can refer, in turn, to examples of exact duplication, division, fragmentation, and decomposition.[18] A character may see just one of his personality traits embodied by another at the same time that other of his traits are embodied in more characters. In sum, doubling by no means refers to a constant, but is nonetheless useful a term.

Textual multiplicity is my own term to explain the presence--real or feigned—of more than one text within a work. The current popular term "intertextuality" in some ways would be more acceptable since at least the term already exists in critical vocabulary.[19] However, that there continues to be widespread disagreement over the very definition and therefore a lack of specific guidelines for isolating and interpreting its suspected presence in a text, is reason enough to seek a term of more utility.

For my purposes, textual multiplicity covers the fact that *Siervo libre de amor*, for example, consists of a frame story and a complete narrative within the work, whose separateness is further underscored by the fact that the frame is first-person narration and the embedded narrative is in the third person.

Since these terms can occasionally refer to the same feature within a work, which could be confusing if the reader thinks that I mean them to be absolute terms, let me give an example here.

In *Grimalte y Gradissa*, Boccacio's *Fiammetta* has been reworked to fit into Flores' literary design. Flores makes the Boccaccian characters

---

[17] See Frye, *The Secular Scripture*, especially Chapter 4, "The Bottomless Dream: Themes of Descent."

[18] (Detroit: Wayne State University Press, 1970), pp. 1-17.

[19] The term intertextuality is generally credited to Julia Kristeva, but a sensible and generally helpful discussion of the concept and its usefulness and limitations can be found in Jonathan Culler's *The Pursuit of Signs: Semiotics, Literature, Deconstruction* (Ithaca: Cornell University Press, 1981). See especially Chapter 5, "Presupposition and Intertextuality," pp. 100-18.

come to life in his own work, but he maintains their literary nature as well by having his female protagonist, Gradissa, read Fiammetta/Fiometa's autobiography before Fiometa and Pamphilo actually appear in the present story. This is a case of textual multiplicity but, in this instance, it also results in a binary structure of the romance, two love stories to be resolved, one hinging on the outcome of the other, and a doubling of characters. The reader constantly moves from an awareness of literature to the idea that what he is reading is an account of real life, and back to the realization that it is, after all, a literary endeavor. It is binary because the plot revolves around two pairs of lovers and their respective love stories. The aspect of doubling is here, not just in the sense of two sets of lovers, but because the characters become doubles of each other and the affections become confused: at one point Grimalte seems to have taken over Pamphilo's role of Fiometa's defender as if he were the lover, and Gradissa accepts Fiometa's lot in life as a mirror of her own destiny. In addition, the binarism of courtly, or frustrated, and physical love affairs is prevalent in each of the works studied here.

*Love and the Idea of Cosmic Degeneration: Thematic Considerations*

In the appendix "Prophecies of Catastrophe and the Emergence of a New World Order," Roger Boase cites some examples of European messianic predictions and expectations. He refers to an apocalyptic hundred-year period which was supposed to have begun in 1385. Francesc Eiximenis predicted "that by the year 1400 all Christian kingdoms would have been destroyed save that of France."[20] In general, when Spanish writers made political predictions, they named Spanish leaders who would emerge victorious in a shake-up of world order. Juan de Mena's *Laberinto de Fortuna*, in which Juan II of Castile is described as a political redeemer, is a good example of this. Among others who acclaimed Juan II was Ruy Páez de Ribera:

> The idea of cosmic degeneration is expressed by several poets in the *Cancionero de Baena*, but it is usually accompanied by a vision of regeneration. Ruy Páez de Ribera, who was writing during the regency of Fernando de Antequera, lists the names of the old nobility and predicts that, with the help of the child king Juan II, these families will recover their former estates:

---

[20] Boase, *The Troubadour Revival*, p. 161. Further references to this book will be given parenthetically in the text of the chapter.

> Perdieron la fuerça de los sus caballos por el rrodamiento del
> mundo aborrido, e agora por este señor que es nasçido los vienes
> perdidos tornáronse a ellos. (pp. 163-64)

In this section Boase does not mention Spanish writers who considered love as a degenerative force, although in an earlier chapter, "Documents on the Troubadour Revival," he gives a selection translated from an anonymous essay on love's properties from the *Cancionero de Herberay* in which love's contradictions are outlined and love's joys heralded. There appears to be hope, according to the writer, that love's ultimate joy results from a concord of wills, but this is difficult to achieve:

> These, Master Hugo, are the laws related to your question which Love is in the habit of observing. It is true that occasionally through slovenliness, excessive appetites, mad obsessions, or because Love wishes to display his might, they are sometimes interrupted, yet it is still firmly maintained that love cannot derive very much strength from one party alone. (p. 150)

Returning to the examples in the appendix, Boase cites John Gower who, in one part of his *Vox clamantis*, supports a theory of universal degeneration yet elsewhere indicates his belief that love is "a remedy for social ills and a Phoenix in the wilderness" (p. 163). This seems to Boase to be contradictory, but he recognizes a possible resolution in the consideration of this paradoxical view of love from *Vox clamantis* as the creator and, at the same time, resolver of all contraries:

> Non amor unicolor est set contrarius in se,
> Qui sine temperie temperat esse vices...
> Est amor iniustus iudex, adversa maritans
> Rerum naturas degenerare facit...
> Mors vivens, vita moriens, discordia concors. (p. 163)

In terms of a prevailing mood of apocalyptic premonitions within Spain, E. Michael Gerli offers the example of Alonso Martínez de Toledo's *Corbacho*, whose "millenarian foreboding is undoubtedly rooted in the sermon tradition."[21] This tradition, Gerli explains, drew

---

21 *Alonso Martínez de Toledo*, TWAS, 398 (Boston: Twayne, 1976), pp. 101-04 at p. 101. Another example of the mood of apocalypse is the anonymous fifteenth-century *Libro de la consolación de España*. ed. Julio Rodríguez-Puértolas, in *Miscelánea de Textos Medievales*, I (Barcelona: Universidad, 1972), pp. 189-212, especially pp. 204-05, where the text specifically refers to the dangers of love.

much material from the evils of society and the sense of impending doom, of the end of the world. A point of contact, of course, between the *Corbacho* and the sentimental romances, is the emphasis on love as the degenerative force or the sin that destroys society.

In the analyses of the sentimental romances, most notably *Estoria de dos amadores, Grisel y Mirabella, Grimalte y Gradissa*, and *Cárcel de Amor*, and, to a lesser extent, *Arnalte y Lucenda*, we saw that the love affair between two people can break the boundaries of individual concerns and extend itself, often in a destructive manner, to those around the lovers, thus disturbing either the natural order or the order of society. The desires of the individual and the rights of society conflict in these cases. Scaglione emphasizes love as man's birthright and how it is employed in literature as symbolic of all of man's natural, individual rights.[22] What the sentimental romances consider, however, is what happens when the individual's desire, in spite of its seeming naturalness, proves to be harmful to the individual himself and society in general. The findings of Evelyn Birge Vitz, mentioned earlier in this chapter, convincingly show how man is unfortunately not the best judge of what he needs, and that what he wants, or desires, is often in conflict with what he needs.

Of the romances examined in this book, four best exemplify the authorial consciousness of the effects of love on the social fabric and not just the individual: *Grisel y Mirabella, Grimalte y Gradissa, Arnalte y Lucenda* and *Cárcel de Amor*. These four end with pessimistic outlooks or false resolutions. Whereas the other works also claim to show the deleterious effects of love, they are not as solutionless or boundless as these four. *Estoria de dos amadores* fits this category, but presents a very different picture from the other works, as we shall see.

Before examining the aforementioned romances, it is important to consider the case of Juan de Flores' romance *Triumpho de Amor*. My tentative conclusion, that it is an allegorical and purportedly historical, though obviously fictitious, account of Love, sets this work apart from the other romances inasmuch as they deal with individuals and their love affairs.[23] It has more in common with them, however, if we move away from the particulars of plot and toward broader concerns.

[22] Aldo D. Scaglione, *Nature and Love in the Late Middle Ages* (Berkeley: University of California Press, 1963).

[23] See my article, "Juan de Flores' Other Work: Technique and Genre of *Triumpho de Amor*," *JHP*, 5 (1980-81), 25-40.

Like its politico-literary counterparts of apocalyptic predictions, *Triumpho de Amor* documents the author as witness to a jumbling of world order in which the God of Love emerges as the one, supreme, heavenly and earthly monarch. Envious fortune sows discord after this victory causing men and women, discontented with their traditional roles in the love process, to petition for change. The God of Love reverses their roles, making women the pursuers and the men, the passive lovers. The author tells of his reluctance to return to Spain with news of this new order, but ultimately decides that he must do so.

There could not be a clearer case of a literary and social process incorporating and paralleling the contemporary political mood. While the exact date of *Triumpho de Amor* is unknown, there is no doubt that it falls within a certain time period, the hundred-year apocalyptic period, placing it, along with the sentimental romances considered here, within the time frame of the political works which considered degeneration and visions of regeneration.

*Estoria de dos amadores*, contained within *Siervo libre de amor*, does not stop with a tale of two lovers who die but continues to include the redefinition of their tomb from a secular resting place to a shrine and, finally, the center of a thriving metropolis. The elements of degeneration are there: when the King kills his son's pregnant lover, provoking the son's subsequent suicide, both the natural world and the courts of the world express their horror and dismay. The Emperor unites the courts in their universal condemnation of the King and his actions, declaring him to be "nuestro capital enemigo" and evoking promises of support from the other courts:

> Luego por todo el Ymperio, sus reynos, ducados, condados, prinçipados y tierras, mandó aclarar ser contrario, capital enemigo del rey Croes de Mondoya, haziendo juras, votos, promessas, de vengar la tan syn piedat muerte que el lleno de toda crueldat asy diera a la ynoçente Lyessa, no haziendo mención los pregones, trompetas, reys darmas y parseuantes de la enemistat de la cruel y sentible muerte que el su buen amigo Ardanlier... (pp. 99-100)

Earlier, upon witnessing the murder of Liessa and then Ardanlier's suicide, nature went wild:

> El dessentydo Lamidoras... dando los grandes gritos, al son de los quales los cauallos atados no sufren las fuertes cadenas; los treze canes quebrantan las fuertes prisiones; las lyndas aves de rrapinia quebrantan las lonjas con las pyhuelas, solas dexan las alcándaras, e

çercan de todas partes los dos cuerpos inanimables que, no passan-
do la hora, vieran respirar. E de la una parte muy fuerte plañiendo
el affortunado ayo, e de la otra relynchando, hasyendo en áspero
los bryosos cauallos, e avllando los bravos alanos con los ventores;
los caçadoras aves batyendo sus alas en rrezyos surtes, tomándose
vnas a otras, fue grande el temor, el triste son de los alarydos, que
el mundo pensó fenecer. (pp. 95-96)

Through the love and loyalty of two people, Lamidoras and the
princess Yrena, for the dead lovers, and later, the appearance of
Macías, the lover *par excellence*, to break the enchantment of the tomb,
Ardanlier and Liessa's deaths are avenged and even greater good
awaits them: they attract pilgrims whose reverence for the lovers
causes them to go on pilgrimages to the tomb/shrine and subsequently settle near the shrine. So many people are drawn there, in
fact, that a city grows up around the shrine.

It seems clear that in portraying the avenging of the lovers, the
author goes above and beyond the call of duty in order to establish
the lovers' goodness. That Macías would defend them would seem to
be enough of a vindication and justification of the love between
Ardanlier and Liessa. But Rodríguez del Padrón proceeds to make a
statement about the power of love and its positive effect on society as
the catalyst for productivity and growth. Considering it in its relation
to the idea of cosmic degeneration, *Estoria de dos amadores* is a very good
example of the social fabric torn asunder and re-established in a
universally understandable, valuable way.

The chapter on *Grisel y Mirabella* outlined the system set up by
Flores—the interplay of love and justice—which I concluded to be a
system undermined by the author himself. Although the women of
the court are the ostensible victors in having avenged the death of the
princess Mirabella by the murder of the misogynist Torrellas, we can
see that the victory is dubious. The women became animal-like and
lost all sense of reason and dignity.

More important, in terms of my conclusions about these romances
in general, is the open-endedness of the text in spite of the seeming
conclusion.[24] The analysis of *Grisel y Mirabella* shows it to be a text of

---

[24] Daniel Eisenberg, "The Pseudo-Historicity of the Romances of Chivalry," *QIA*, nos. 45-46 (1976), 253-59, shows that open-endedness, or inconclu-
siveness, is a device employed by the authors of romances of chivalry in order
to increase the sense that this is history, true events which do not necessarily
have conclusions. The same device was employed by authors of sentimental
romances.

increasing chaos and violence in which violence seems to have gained a momentum of its own, outside the characters' control. It is unlikely, therefore, that the violence stopped with the death of Torrellas even though the printed word ended there. In addition to this projected continuum of violence, all the male-female relationships in the text have been destroyed, the justice system is shown to be ineffective in the face of such violence and, ultimately, the society/court has split into two opposing groups of men and women, a polarization which limits, or even eliminates, the effective functioning of society.

As an example of cosmic degeneration, *Grimalte y Gradissa* falls somewhere in-between *Grisel y Mirabella* and *Cárcel de Amor*. It approaches *Cárcel de Amor* in that its violence and the dissolution of relationships is more contained than in *Grisel y Mirabella*: here, death comes only to one of the main characters and does not appear to extend itself to the destruction of others and the definitive polarization of men and women. In *Cárcel de Amor* the notion of natural order gone awry comes from the combination of the chain of events caused by desire— "tu hermosura causó el afición, y el afición el deseo, y el deseo la pena, y la pena el atrevimiento"—with the mother's soliloquy which accuses love of provoking disorder, here, the death of one so young. In *Grisel y Mirabella* cosmic or social degeneration is implied by the increasing momentum of violence and the widening web of participants in that violence.

*Grimalte y Gradissa* neither involves all of society in its evolution nor does there appear a monologue with the poignancy and anguish of a Pleberio or Leriano's mother. Nevertheless, the work indeed deals with the idea of social change and destruction of known patterns of behavior.

First of all, in the relationship of the four protagonists, we can see a microcosm of society. Society consists not of isolated beings, but of a network of interdependence and interaction. Gradissa learns of Fiometa's plight and realizes that abandonment by the successful lover is a very real danger for one and all. Her insistence that Grimalte attempt to reconcile the lovers initiates a web of dependency among the characters.

Secondly, references are made throughout the text to "nuevas invenciones" and "nuevas leyes." Grimalte is astonished that Pamphilo so cavalierly abandons what Grimalte perceives to be the lover's duty with regard to the beloved. He cannot understand Pamphilo's disregard for Fiometa:

Pareçe que nuevas leyes usays en amor, en querer y consentir que
aquella tan sin errores assi moriesse por vos; que mas razonable cosa
es, como suele acaheçer, a nosotros hombres morir por las mujeres.
(p. 58)

Reference to "nuevas leyes" implies a kind of universality that precedes
the story of these four people. Laws develop not out of a void but out
of a need to regulate and codify desirable or undesirable behavior. We
suspect that Grimalte refers to a courtly code of love, one which
permits a certain continuity and stability of behavior in terms of
defined rules for men and women. Pamphilo's hardheartedness and
refusal to return to Fiometa provokes her suicide. When Grimalte
prevails upon Pamphilo to realize the error of his ways, Pamphilo's
only recourse for repentance is exile from society and abandonment of
normal human behavior: he walks on all fours, lives in a cave, refuses
to speak once Grimalte has tracked him down, and subsists on green
grass. Grimalte's subsequent acceptance of this mental and social exile
brings to three out of four the number of lovers who are no longer
normally functioning members of society.

In addition to Pamphilo and Grimalte's exile in an undesirable,
unidentifiable world, Fiometa's nocturnal vists in the company of devils
who torture her are intrusions of the ever-frightening "other world"
on our own known world. In his discussion of the cosmos, the
sacredness of "our world," Eliade says: "Our cosmos, our world is
contrasted with the other world, foreign chaotic space peopled by
ghosts, demons, 'foreigners' (who are assimilated to demons and the
souls of the dead)."[25]

*Grimalte y Gradissa* is a study of reason and will, in which only one of
the four protagonists, Gradissa, exercises an admirable use of reason.
The work also shows the disintegration of a social group, traceable
initially to love and desire, and fueled by willful ignorance of reason
until the ending where the world has no recognizable normalcy.

*Cárcel de Amor* ends with the lament of Leriano's mother over the
imminent death of her son, and the author's recounting of Leriano's
final words: "Acabados son mis males" (p. 176). The similarity between
the mother's lament and the ending of *La Celestina*, Pleberio's *planctus* on
the death of his daughter, has been noted.

[25] Mircea Eliade, *The Sacred and the Profane: The Nature of Religion*, trans. Willard
R. Trask (New York: Harcourt, Brace and World, 1959; rpt. Harcourt Brace
Jovanovich, n.d.), pp. 47-48.

Pleberio not only laments his personal loss, but questions his own world view and sense of justice. It seems that inconstancy is the only thing that can be counted on, that there is no just order, nothing stable. The last line of his lament, "¿Por qué me dejaste triste y solo in *hac lachrymarum valle?*," is a cry of despair, an unanswered or unanswerable question which results in a kind of open-ended text:

> Pleberio is left behind, in total temporal and physical isolation... The past, retrievable only through memory, disappears in pain. The future exists no longer for Pleberio, least responsible for but most punished by the inescapable destruction of time. The present must end when dialogue is cut off and monologue fails. The microcosm of humanity and time has destroyed itself in *La Celestina*, leaving Pleberio "triste e solo in hac lachrymarum valle." When his monologue in the void ends, Pleberio too disappears without a trace.[26]

Pleberio's last words, a quotation from Psalm 83, are an ironic use of the consolatory nature of the words, suggesting perhaps the inability of consolatory writings to console, or, going a step further, the inability of religion to console. What is certain here is that Pleberio uses a particular series of events in order to focus on the wider implications of those events: they serve to point out the invalidity of our perceptions of a just, natural order.

Leriano's mother's lament, on the one hand, gives the text an open-endedness similar to that of *Celestina*: the story—that Leriano ultimately does die—is less important than the question that his death provokes. On the other hand, the lament serves as a structural counterpoint to Laureola's mother's lament to her imprisoned daughter. There are similarities: the Queen expresses her disbelief that the judicial process could result in a verdict of guilt, when it seems to her, at least, that the testimony of Laureola's natural evidence of purity and innocence should counteract the verbal testimony of her accusers. Leriano's mother laments the injustice of nature—be it named fortune, fate, or love—that would cause a young man's death, but permit an old woman to live. Both mothers fear that their children's death and their own continued life comes as punishment for their personal sins. What greater punishment than to see one's children die? Laureola's innocence is ultimately recognized—the judicial process reverses its deci-

---

[26] Dorothy Sherman Severin, *Memory in "La Celestina"* (London: Tamesis, 1970), p. 52.

sion—but her life irrevocably changes. She fears that subsequent involvement with Leriano would cause the earlier charges to be resurrected and reevaluated—to her detriment. Leriano, because of all this, is still subject—willfully or not—to what seems to his mother to be an unnatural order of things.

One can see a similarity here to the issue of love and justice in *Grisel y Mirabella*: man-created justice, a system of laws, makes mistakes but instinctual justice, revenge outside the law, is not necessarily superior to this.

Leriano suffers from melancholy, a recognized and occasionally fatal illness, as Whinnom tells us.[27] This love-sickness causes the victim to relinquish his grasp of reason and succumb to the destructive powers of love. Leriano himself regarded the process as a chain whose end is death:

> Podrás dezir que cómo pensé escrevirte; no te maravilles, que tu hermosura causó el afición, y el afición el deseo, y el deseo la pena, y la pena el atrevimiento, y si porque lo hize te pareciere que merezco muerte, mándamela dar, que muy mejor es morir por tu causa que bevir sin tu esperança, y hablándote verdad, la muerte; sin que tú me la dieses yo mismo me la daría, por hallar en ella la libertad que en la vida busco, si tú no hovieses de quedar infamada por matadora. (p. 99)

Leriano's mother rails against love and fortune, not against Leriano, so we know that she must regard his sufferings as out of his control and in the hands of a capricious fortune, against which we are defenseless since the nature of fortune's contrariness is such that our perceptions of natural order are destroyed.

*Tractado de amores de Arnalte y Lucenda* is less violently dramatic than the other works, yet it clearly belongs in this category. In *Arnalte y Lucenda*, desire inspired jealousy, which gave rise to violence—the death of Elierso. This, in turn, led to Lucenda's retreat to a convent, completely shutting Arnalte out of her life. Arnalte prays to the Virgin Mary, but finds solace nowhere, not even in religion:

> Pues como las angustias así acabase, por el desmerescer mío no merescí de Nuestra Señora ser oído; y como viese que en Dios ni en

---

[27] Keith Whinnom, introduction to *Cárcel de Amor*, pp. 13-15, discusses the idea, common in late medieval medical treatises, of love-melancholy as a real sickness.

ellas ni en las gentes remedio no fallava, de verme donde gentes ver
no me pudiesen determiné. (p. 166)

Arnalte fears leaving his sister behind, but his appeal to the king
has happy results in an arranged marriage for Belisa. She will be
included in court society as a wife even though her brother sees no
recourse for himself but exile. He and his friends or servants withdraw
from society to where they dwell in a place of "estraña soledad."

*Arnalte y Lucenda*, then, ends in a fragmented society with no
proposed solutions. This text, unlike the others, is open-ended not so
much due to its lack of solution, or resolution, but to the sense of the
telling and retelling of the tale that comes from its inherent circularity.
At the end of the story we are right back in the woods where the story
began and the author, advised by Arnalte to carry the story away with
him and use it as a lesson, does so, and we are reading the fruit of that
effort.

## *Flowers of Grass: Didactic Considerations*

*Siervo libre de amor, Triste deleytación* and *Processo de cartas de amores*, while
differing somewhat in the treatment of secular love, are alike in their
conclusions that there is a higher love, the love of God, which is
stronger than earthly love and, most important of all, is eternal. Just as
in the Bible earthly love is not condemned or forbidden, it is not
condemned here. Illustrated instead are the possible undesirable consequences and the potential dangers, both spiritual and physical. But
the dichotomy of earthly love/love of God is not labeled evil and good,
but good and better. These Biblical verses explain the idea:

> Seeing ye have purified your souls in obeying the truth through the
> Spirit unto unfeigned love of the brethren, see that ye love one
> another with a pure heart fervently:

> Being born again, not of corruptible seed, but of incorruptible, by
> the word of God, which liveth and abideth for ever.

> For all flesh is as grass, and all the glory of man as the flower of
> grass. The grass withereth, and the flower thereof falleth away:

> But the word of the Lord endureth forever. (I Peter, 1:22-25)

One may find a more contemporary reference than the Bible,
however, in order to prove the point that love can be seen in terms of
benefits by degree rather than in simple ones of right and wrong. Since

the people often regarded love as an illness or madness, it is not surprising to find this in a fifteenth-century scientific treatise, López de Villalobos' *Epílogo en medicina*:

> Si el amor que tienes plantado en la mujer
> ó en las otras cosas mundanas le arrancas
> de allí y le trasplantas en Dios, tú
> granjearás un árbol de vida y de sabiduría,
> y gozarías de un fructo sin comparación
> y provechoso.[28]

These works show how the memory and fame of love outlive mortal life. But the love of God, assuring the soul's eternal happiness, is the best pursuit of all.

It is interesting to note that these three works are more clearly divided in terms of narrative style than the other romances. They are so neatly divided, in fact, that one, *Siervo libre de amor*, is normally summed up with little mention and even less analysis of its intercalated, central narrative, *Estoria de dos amadores*, while another, *Processo de cartas de amores*, is usually discussed (and even published and edited) as a separate work from its other half, *Quexa y aviso contra el Amor(Luzindaro y Medusina)*. *Triste deleytación*, recently edited for the first time, will no doubt not suffer the same fate of amputation since, although the work is clearly divided into two parts, the same protagonist continues in both.

In *Siervo libre de amor* Siervo takes heart from his realized heritage with Macías, the greatest, most loyal lover of all time. The lesson Siervo learns is loyalty—he has been a loyal lover and loyalty must have its rewards, as we learn from the story of Ardanlier, Liessa, Yrena and Lamidoras. Siervo's own love experience was bitter, as we know from the recounting of it and from the poetry subsequent to *Estoria de dos amadores*. Earthly love, unequivocally not condemned in *Estoria de dos amadores*, will not be the route for Siervo. The love of God, "Servid al señor," the birds tell him, will sustain him.

*Triste deleytación* shows how earthly love can be subjugated to a higher love. La Señora has entered a convent and, upon discovering this, El Enamorado, too, renounces the world, although, we are told, he occasionally is plagued by remembrances of his love for La Señora. The author does not condemn earthly love: El Enamorado visits the hell,

---

[28] *Curiosidades bibliográficas*, ed. Adolfo de Castro, Biblioteca de Autores Españoles, 36 (Madrid: M. Rivadeneyra, 1855), pp. 491-92.

purgatory, and paradise of lovers. Some lovers receive praise, others suffer their deserved punishments. But instead of this being a solutionless text or one which ends in death, the love of God comes through as a viable path to follow. That it is not a total consolation is true, but at least there appears to be life after love, and a life which will bring eternal love and life.

*Processo de cartas de amores*, viewed as an entity, advocates a life devoted to God. *Quexa y aviso* ends with poetry that disparages the lures of earthly love and promotes the value of spirituality. The lovers, Luzindaro and Medusina, are not themselves condemned, but their story exposes the deceptions of love and false promises of eternity. As a lesson to the inconsolable Captivo of the first part, *Processo de cartas*, he will see that it is better in the long run to turn his thoughts from his beloved and set his sights on a higher, more permanent goal.

# Selected Bibliography

## A. Primary Sources

*El cancionero de Palacio (manuscrito Nº 594)*. Ed. Francisca Vendrell de Millás. Barcelona: CSIC, 1945.

*Cancionero general de Hernando del Castillo*. Ed. José Antonio Balenchana. Sociedad de Bibliófilos Españoles, 21. Madrid: 1882.

*Le chansonnier espagnol d'Herberay des Essarts (XVᵉ siècle)*. Ed. Charles V. Aubrun. Bordeaux: Féret, 1951.

*Curiosidades Bibliográficas*. Ed. Adolfo de Castro. BAE, 36. Madrid: Rivadeneyra, 1855.

*Dos opúsculos isabelinos: "La coronación de la señora Gracisla" (BN MS. 22020) y Nicolás Núñez, "Cárcel de Amor."* Ed. Keith Whinnom. Exeter Hispanic Texts, 22. Exeter: University, 1979.

Flores, Juan de. *Grimalte y Gradissa*. Ed. Pamela Waley. London: Tamesis, 1971.

Lucena, Luis de. *Repetición de amores*. Ed. Jacob Ornstein. University of North Carolina Studies in Romance Languages and Literatures, 23. Chapel Hill: University Press, 1954.

Matulka, Barbara. *The Novels of Juan de Flores and Their European Diffusion: A Study in Comparative Literature*. New York: Institute of French Studies, 1931.

Mena, Juan de. *El laberinto de Fortuna o las trescientas*. Ed. José Manuel Blecua. Clásicos Castellanos, 119. Madrid: Espasa-Calpe, 1943; rpt. 1968.

—————. *Obra lírica*. Ed. Miguel Angel Pérez Priego. Madrid: Alhambra, 1979.

*Miscelánea de Textos Medievales*, I. Ed. Julio Rodríguez-Puértolas. Barcelona: Universidad, 1972.

Pedro, Condestable de Portugal. *Sátira de felice e infelice vida*. In *Opúsculos literarios de los siglos XIV a XVI*. Ed. Antonio Paz y Melia. Sociedad de Bibliófilos Españoles, 29. Madrid: 1892, pp. 47-101.

Rodríguez del Padrón, Juan. *Obras de Juan Rodríguez de la Cámara (o del Padrón)*. Ed. Antonio Paz y Melia. Sociedad de Bibliófilos Españoles, 22. Madrid 1884.

—————. *Siervo libre de amor*. Introd. Antonio Prieto. Ed. Francisco Serrano Puente. Clásicos Castalia, 66. Madrid: Castalia, 1976.

Ruiz, Juan. *Libro de buen amor*. Ed. and trans. Raymond S. Willis. Princeton: University Press, 1972.

San Pedro, Diego de. *Obras completas*, I: *Tractado de amores de Arnalte y Lucenda y Sermón*. Ed. Keith Whinnom. Clásicos Castalia, 54. Madrid: Castalia, 1973.

————. *Obras completas*, II: *Cárcel de Amor*. Ed. Keith Whinnom. Clásicos Castalia, 39. Madrid: Castalia, 1971.

————. *Obras completas*, III: *Poesías*. Ed. Keith Whinnom and Dorothy Sherman Severin. Clásicos Castalia, 98. Madrid: Castalia, 1979.

Segura, Juan de. *Processo de cartas de amores: A Critical and Annotated Edition of the First Epistolary Novel (1548) together with an English Translation*. Ed. and trans. Edwin B. Place. Northwestern University Studies, Humanities Series, 23. Evanston, Ill: Northwestern University Press, 1950.

————. *Processo de cartas de amores y Quexa y aviso contra Amor por Juan de Segura y otras obras*. Ed. Joaquín del Val. Sociedad de Bibliófilos Españoles, new series, 31. Madrid: 1956.

*Triste deleytaçión: An Anonymous Fifteenth-Century Castilian Romance*. Ed. E. Michael Gerli. Washington: Georgetown University Press, 1982.

*Triste deleytaçión*. Ed. Regula Rohland de Langbehn. Madrid: Fundación Universitaria Española, 1984.

Urrea, Pedro Manuel de. *Penitençia de amor*. Ed. R. Foulché-Delbosc. Bibliotheca Hispanica, 10. Barcelona: L'Avenç, 1902.

## B. Secondary Sources

Andrachuk, Gregory Peter. "The Function of the *Estoria de dos amadores* within the *Siervo libre de amor*." *RCEH*, 2 (1977-78), 27-38.

————."A Further Look at Italian Influence in the *Siervo libre de amor*."*JHP*, 6 (1981-82), 45-56.

————. "On the Missing Third Part of *Siervo libre de amor*." *HR*, 45 (1977), 171-80.

Bastianutti, D. L. "La función de la Fortuna en la primera novela sentimental española." *RN*, 14 (1972-73), 394-402.

Boase, Roger. *The Origin and Meaning of Courtly Love: A Critical Study of European Scholarship*. Manchester: University Press, 1977.

————. *The Troubadour Revival: A Study of Traditionalism and Social Change in Late Medieval Spain*. London: Routledge and Kegan Paul, 1978.

Bogin, Meg, ed. and trans. *The Women Troubadors*. New York: Paddington Press, 1976.

Brownlee, Marina Scordilis. "The Generic Status of the *Siervo libre de amor*: Rodríguez del Padrón's Reworking of Dante." *PoT*, 5, no. 3 (1984), 629-43.

Campa, Pedro F. "The Spanish Tristán: Research and New Directions." *Tristania*, 3, no. 2 (May 1978), 36-45.

Castro Guisasola, F. *Observaciones sobre las fuentes literarias de "La Celestina*." Anejos de la *RFE*, 5. Madrid: Centro de Estudios Históricos, 1924.

Chorpenning, Joseph F. "Rhetoric and Feminism in the *Cárcel de Amor*." *BHS*, 54 (1977), 1-8.

Cirot, Georges. "Le 'Cautivo' de Cervantes et Notre-Dame de Liesse." *BH*, 38 (1936), 378-82.

Cocozzella, Peter. "The Thematic Unity of Juan Rodríguez del Padrón's *Siervo libre de amor*." *Hispania*, 64 (1981), 188-98.

Corfis, Ivy A. "The *Dispositio* of Diego de San Pedro's *Cárcel de Amor.*" *Ibero-romania*, 21 (1985), 32-47.

Corominas, Joan. *Diccionario crítico etimológico de la lengua castellana*. Vol. III. Madrid: Gredos, 1956.

Culler, Jontathan. *The Pursuit of Signs: Semiotics, Literature, Deconstruction*. Ithaca: Cornell University Press, 1981.

Cvitanovič, Dinko. "El tratadismo en Juan Rodríguez del Padrón." *Cuadernos del Sur*, 11 (1969-71), 25-36.

——————.*La novela sentimental española*. El Soto, 21. Madrid: Editorial Prensa Española, 1973.

Damiani, Bruno. "The Didactic Intention of the *Cárcel de Amor.*" *Hispanófila*, no. 56 (Jan. 1976), 29-43.

Denomy, A.J. *The Heresy of Courtly Love*. New York: MacMullen, 1947; rpt. Gloucester, MA: Peter Smith, 1965.

Deyermond, A.D. "El hombre salvaje en la novela sentimental." *Filología*, 10 (1964), 97-111.

——————. *A Literary History of Spain: The Middle Ages*. London: Ernest Benn; New York: Barnes & Noble, 1971.

——————. "The Lost Genre of Medieval Spanish Literature." *HR*, 43 (1975), 231-59.

Dudley, Edward J. "Court and Country: The Fusion of Two Images of Love in Juan Rodríguez's *El siervo libre de amor.*" *PMLA*, 82 (1967), 117-20.

——————. "Structure and Meaning in the Novel of Juan Rodríguez: *Siervo libre de amor.*" Diss. University of Minnesota, 1963.

Dunn, Peter N. "Narrator as Character in the *Cárcel de Amor.*" *MLN*, 94 (1979), 187-99.

Durán, Armando. *Estructura y técnicas de la novela sentimental y caballeresca*. Madrid: Gredos, 1973.

Earle, Peter G. "Love Concepts in *La Cárcel de Amor* and *La Celestina.*" *Hispania*, 39 (1956), 92-96.

Eisenberg, Daniel. "The Pseudo-Historicity of the Romances of Chivalry." *QIA*, nos. 45-46 (1974-75), 253-59.

Eliade, Mircea. *The Sacred and the Profane: The Nature of Religion*. Trans. Willard R. Trask. New York: Harcourt, Brace and World, 1959; rpt. Harcourt Brace Jovanovich, n. d.

Fernández Jiménez, Juan. "Amor cortés en el *Tratado notable de amor.*" *ExTL*, 10, no. 1 (Fall 1981), 23-26.

——————. "La estructura del *Siervo libre de amor* y la crítica reciente." *CHA*, #388 (1982), 178-90.

——————. "*Siervo libre de amor*: ¿novela incompleta?." *Hispanófila*, no. 75 (May 1982), 1-7.

Fleischman, Suzanne. "Dialectic Structures in *Flamenca.*" *RF*, 92 (1980), 223-46.

Forcione, Alban K. *Cervantes and the Humanist Vision: A Study of Four "Exemplary Novels."* Princeton: University Press, 1982.

——————. *Cervantes, Aristotle and the "Persiles."* Princeton: University Press, 1970.

——————.*Cervantes' Christian Romance: A Study of "Persiles y Sigismunda."* Princeton: University Press, 1972.

Frye, Northrop. *The Secular Scripture: A Study of the Structure of Romance*. Cambridge, MA: Harvard University Press, 1976; rpt. 1978.

Gargano, Antonio. "Stato attuale degli studi sulla 'novela sentimental.' 1. La questione del genere." *SIs*, (1979), 59-80.

————."Stato attuale degli studi sulla 'novela sentimental.' 2. Juan Rodríguez del Padrón, Diego de San Pedro, Juan de Flores." *SIs*, (1980), 39-69.

Gascón-Vera, Elena. "La ambigüedad en el concepto del amor y de la mujer en la prosa castellana del siglo XV." *BRAE*, 59 (1979), 119-55.

Gatti, José Francisco. *Contribución al estudio de la "Cárcel de Amor": La apología de Leriano*. Buenos Aires: n.p., 1955.

Gerli, E. Michael. *Alfonso Martínez de Toledo*. TWAS, 398. Boston: Twayne, 1976.

————. "Leriano's Libation: Notes on the *Cancionero* Lyric, *Ars Moriendi*, and the Probable Debt to Boccaccio." *MLN*, 96 (1981), 414-20.

Gilderman, Martin S. *Juan Rodríguez de la Cámara*. TWAS, 423. Boston: Twayne, 1977.

Girard, René. *Deceit, Desire and the Novel: Self and Other in Literary Structure*. Trans. Yvonne Freccero. Baltimore: Johns Hopkins University Press, 1966; rpt. 1980.

————. "Myth and Ritual in Shakespeare: *A Midsummer Night's Dream*." In *Textual Strategies: Perspectives in Post-Structuralist Criticism*. Ed. Josué V. Harari. Ithaca: Cornell University Press, 1979; rpt. 1984, pp. 189-212.

————."*To Double Business Bound:*" *Essays on Literature, Mimesis, and Anthropology*. Baltimore: Johns Hopkins University Press, 1978.

————.*Violence and the Sacred*. Trans. Patrick Gregory. Baltimore: Johns Hopkins University Press, 1977; rpt. 1979.

Green, Otis H. "Juan de Mena in the Sixteenth Century: Additional Data." *HR*, 21 (1953), 138-40.

Grieve, Patricia E. "Juan de Flores' Other Work: Technique and Genre of *Triumpho de Amor*." *JHP*, 5 (1980-81), 25-40.

————. "Anachronism in the work of a 'Careless' Counterfeiter: The Case of Juan de Segura." Forthcoming.

Guillén, Claudio. *Literature as System: Essays Toward the Theory of Literary History*. Princeton: University Press, 1971.

Hernández Alonso, César. *"Siervo libre de amor" de Juan Rodríguez del Padrón*. Valladolid: Universidad, 1970.

Herrero, Javier. "The Allegorical Structure of the *Siervo libre de amor*." *Speculum*, 55 (1980), 751-64.

Huizinga, J. *The Waning of the Middle Ages: A Study of the Forms of Life, Thought and Art in France and the Netherlands in the Fourteenth and Fifteenth Centuries*. 1924; rpt. Doubleday Anchor Books. Garden City, N.Y.: Doubleday, 1954.

Hunt, Tony. "The Structure of Medieval Narrative." *JES*, 3 (1973), 295-328.

Impey, Olga Tudorică. "The Literary Emancipation of Juan Rodríguez del Padrón: From the Fictional 'Cartas' to the *Siervo libre de amor*." *Speculum*, 55 (1980), 305-16.

————. "Ovid, Alfonso X, and Juan Rodríguez del Padrón: Two Castilian Translations of the *Heroides* and the Beginnings of Spanish Sentimental Prose." *BHS*, 57 (1980), 283-97.

Kany, Charles E. *The Beginnings of the Epistolary Novel in France, Italy and Spain.* University of California Publications in Modern Philology, 21, part 1. Berkeley: University of California Press, 1937.

Kassier, Theodore L. "*Cancionero* Poetry and *La Celestina*: From Metaphor to Reality." *Hispanófila*, no. 56 (Jan 1976), 1-28.

Kermode, Frank. *The Sense of an Ending: Studies in the Theory of Fiction.* London: Oxford University Press, 1966; rpt. 1979.

Krause, Anna. "El 'tractado' novelístico de Diego de San Pedro." *BH*, 54 (1952), 245-75.

Kurtz, Barbara E. "Diego de San Pedro's *Cárcel de Amor* and the Tradition of the Allegorical Edifice." *JHP*, 8 (1983-84), 123-38.

Lacy, Norris J. "Spatial Form in Medieval Romance." *YFS*, 51 (1974), 160-69.

Langbehn-Rohland, Regula. *Zur Interpretation der Romane des Diego de San Pedro.* Studia Romanica, 18. Heidelberg: Carl Winter, 1970.

Lewis, C. S. *The Allegory of Love: A Study in Medieval Tradition.* Oxford: Clarendon Press, 1936; rpt. 1977.

Lida [de Malkiel], María Rosa. "La hipérbole sagrada en la poesía castellana del siglo XV." *RFH*, 8 (1946), 121-30.

—————. *Juan de Mena: poeta del prerrenacimiento español.* Publicaciones de la *NRFH*, 1. Mexico City: El Colegio de México, 1950.

—————. "Juan Rodríguez del Padrón: vida y obras." *NRFH*, 6 (1952), 313-51.

—————. "Juan Rodríguez del Padrón: Influencia." *NRFH*, 8 (1954), 1-38.

Lindsay, Jack. *The Troubadours and Their World of the Twelfth and Thirteenth Centuries.* London: Frederick Muller, 1976.

Löseth, E. *Le Roman en Prose de 'Tristan', le roman de Palamède et la compilation de Rusticien de Pise, analyse critique d'aprèsk les manuscrits de Paris.* Bibliothèque de l'Ecole des Hautes Études, 82. Paris, n.p., 1891; rpt. New York: Burt Franklin, 1980.

Lowes, John Livingston. "The Loveres' Maladye of Hereos." *MP*, 11 (1913-14), 491-546.

Mandrell, James. "Author and Authority in *Cárcel de Amor*: The Role of El Auctor." *JHP*, 8 (1983-84), 99-122.

Márquez Villanueva, Francisco. "*Cárcel de Amor*, novela política." *Revista de Occidente*, 2nd series, 14 (1966), 185-200. Rpt. in his *Relecciones de literatura medieval.* Colección de Bolsillo, 54. Seville: Publicaciones de la Universidad de Sevilla, 1977, pp. 75-94.

Martínez Jiménez, José Antonio and Francisco Muñóz Marquina. "Hacia una caracterización del género 'novela sentimental.'" *Nuevo Hispanismo: Revista Crítica de Literatura y Sociedad*, no. 2 (Spring 1982), 11-43.

Martínez-Barbeito, Carlos. *Macías el enamorado y Juan Rodríguez del Padrón.* Biblioteca de Galicia, 4. Santiago de Compostela: Sociedad de Bibliófilos Gallegos, 1951.

Matulka, Barbara. "An Anti-Feminist Treatise of Fifteenth-Century Spain: Lucena's *Repetición de amores.*" *RR*, 22 (1931), 96-116.

Menéndez y Pelayo, Marcelino. *Orígenes de la novela.* Vol., II. 1907; rpt. Madrid: CSIC, 1943.

Morales Blouin, Egla. *El ciervo y la fuente: mito y folklore del agua en la lírica tradicional.* Studia Humanitatis. Madrid: José Porrúa Turanzas, 1981.

Nardi, Bruno. "L'amore e i medici medievali." In *Studi in onore Angelo Monteverdi.* Modena: 1959, pp. 517-42.

Nelson, William. *Fact or Fiction: The Dilemma of the Renaissance Storyteller.* Cambridge, MA: Harvard University Press, 1973.

Nepaulsingh, Colbert I. "Talavera's Imagery and the Structure of the *Corbacho,*" *RCEH,* 4, (1980), 329-49.

Nozick, Martin. "The Inez de Castro Theme in European Literature." *CL,* 3 (1951), 330-41.

Olmsted, Everett Ward. "Story of *Grisel and Mirabella.*" In *Homenaje ofrecido a Menéndez Pidal: Miscelánea de estudios lingüísticos, literarios e históricos.* Vol. II. Madrid: Hernando, 1925, pp. 369-73.

Ornstein, Jacob. "La misoginia y el profeminismo en la literatura castellana." *RFH,* 3 (1941), 219-32.

Praag, J.A. van. "Algo sobre la fortuna de Juan de Flores." *RR,* 26 (1935), 349-50.

Randall, Dale B.J. *The Golden Tapestry: A Critical Survey of Non-Chivalric Spanish Fiction in English Translation (1543-1657).* Durham, N.C.: Duke University Press, 1963.

Rey, Alfonso. "La primera persona narrativa en Diego de San Pedro." *BHS,* 58 (1981), 95-103.

Reynier, Gustave. *Le Roman sentimental avant "L'Astrée."* Paris: Colin, 1908.

Richthofen, Erich von. "Petrarca, Dante y Andreas Capellanus: Fuentes inadvertidas de *La cárcel de amor.*" *RCEH,* 1 (1976-77), 30-38.

Riquer, Martín de. "*Triste deleytaçión:* novela castellana del siglo XV." *RFE,* 40 (1956), 33-65.

Rogers, Katharine M. *The Troublesome Helpmate: A History of Misogyny in Literature.* Seattle: University of Washington Press, 1966.

Rogers, Robert. *A Psychoanalytic Study of the Double in Literature.* Detroit: Wayne State University Press, 1970.

Rolfs, Daniel J. "Dante, Petrarch, Boccaccio and the Problem of Suicide." *RR,* 67 (1976), 200-25.

Rougemont, Denis de. *Love in the Western World.* Trans. Montgomery Belgion. 1956; rpt. New York: Harper and Row, 1974.

Ryding, William W. *Structure in Medieval Narrative.* The Hague: Mouton, 1971.

Samonà, Carmelo. "Diego de San Pedro: dall' *Arnalte e Lucenda* alla *Cárcel de Amor.*" In *Studi in onore di Pietro Silva.* Florence: Felice le Monnier, 1957, pp. 261-77.

Scaglione, Aldo D. *Nature and Love in the Late Middle Ages.* Berkeley: University of California Press, 1963.

Scudieri Ruggiere, Jole. "Un romanzo sentimentale: il *Tratado notable de Amor,* di Juan de Cardona." *RFE,* 46 (1963), 49-79.

Severin, Dorothy Sherman. *Memory in "La Celestina."* London: Tamesis, 1970.

————. "Structure and Thematic Repetitions in Diego de San Pedro's *Cárcel de Amor* and *Arnalte y Lucenda.*" *HR,* 45 (1977), 165-69.

Sewell, Elizabeth. *The Human Metaphor.* Notre Dame: University Press, 1964.

Sharrer, Harvey L. "Letters in the Hispanic *Prose Tristan* Texts: Iseut's Complaint and Tristan's Reply." *Tristania,* 7 (1981-82), 3-20.

————. "Malory and the Spanish and Italian Tristan Texts: The Search for the Missing Link." *Tristania*, 4, no. 2 (May 1979), 36-43.

Shepard, Odell. *The Lore of the Unicorn*. Boston: Houghton Mifflin, 1930.

Stewart, Susan. *Nonsense: Aspects of Intertextuality in Folklore and Literature*. Baltimore: Johns Hopkins University Press, 1979.

Street, Florence. "Hernán Núñez and the Earliest Printed Editions of Mena's *El laberinto de Fortuna*." *MLR*, 61 (1966), 51-63.

Tejerina-Canal, Santiago. "Unidad en *Cárcel de Amor*: el motivo de la tiranía." *KRQ*, 31 (1984), 51-59.

Tórrego, Esther. "Convención retórica y ficción narrativa en la *Cárcel de amor*," *NRFH*, 33 (1983), 330-39.

Utley, Francis Lee. *The Crooked Rib: An Analytical Index to the Argument about Women in English and Scots Literature to the End of the Year 1568*. Columbus: The Ohio State University, 1944.

Van Beysterveldt, Antony. *Amadís-Esplandián-Calisto: Historia de un linaje adulterado*. Madrid: José Porrúa Turanzas, 1982.

————. "La nueva teoría del amor en las novelas de Diego de San Pedro." *CHA*, no. 349 (1979), 70-83.

————. "Revisión de los debates feministas del siglo XV y las novelas de Juan de Flores." *Hispania*, 64 (1981), 1-13.

Varela, José Luis. "Revisión de la novela sentimental." *RFE*, 48 (1965), 351-82.

Vinaver, Eugène. *Form and Meaning in Medieval Romance*. [London]: Modern Humanities Research Association, 1966.

————. *The Rise of Romance*. Oxford: Clarendon Press, 1971.

Vitz, Evelyn Birge. "Desire and Causality in Medieval Narrative." *RR*, 71 (1973), 213-43.

Vossler, Karl. *La soledad en la poesía española*. Trans. José Miguel Sacristán. Madrid: Revista de Occidente, 1941.

Waley, Pamela. "*Cárcel de amor* and *Grisel y Mirabella*: A Question of Priority." *BHS*, 50 (1973), 340-56.

————. "Fiammetta and Pánfilo Continued." *IS*, 24 (1969), 15-31.

————. Juan de Flores and the Evolution of Spanish Fiction in the Fifteenth Century." Diss., Westfield College, University of London, 1968.

————. "Juan de Flores y *Tristán de Leonís*," *Hispanófila*, 12 (1961), 1-14.

————. "Love and Honour in the *Novelas sentimentales* of Diego de San Pedro and Juan de Flores." *BHS*, 43 (1966), 253-75.

Wardropper, Bruce W. "Allegory and the role of 'el Autor' in the *Cárcel de amor*." *PQ*, 31 (1952), 39-44.

————. "El mundo sentimental de la *Cárcel de amor*." *RFE*, 37 (1953), 168-93.

Weissberger, Barbara F. "Authors, Characters and Readers in *Grimalte y Gradissa*." In *Creation and Re-Creation: Experiments in Literary Form in Early Modern Spain*. Eds. Ronald Surtz and Nora Weinerth. Newark, Delaware: Juan de la Cuesta—Hispanic Monographs, 1983, pp. 61-76.

————. "The Role of the *Auctor* in the Spanish Sentimental Novel." Diss., Harvard University, 1976.

Whinnom, Keith. *Diego de San Pedro*. TWAS, 310. New York: Twayne, 1974.

—————. "Diego de San Pedro's Stylistic Reform." *BHS*, 37 (1960), 1-15.

—————. "Hacia una interpretación y apreciación de las canciones del *Cancionero general* de 1511." *Filología*, 13 (1968-69), 361-81.

—————. *La poesía amatoria de la época de los Reyes Católicos*. Durham Modern Languages Series, Hispanic Monographs, 2. Durham: University, 1981.

—————. "The Problem of the 'Best-Seller' in Spanish Golden-Age Literature." *BHS*, 57 (1980), 189-98.

—————. *Spanish Sentimental Historigraphy: Three Forms of Distortion*. Exeter: University, 1967.

—————. *The Spanish Sentimental Romance 1440-1550: A Critical Bibliography*. Research Bibliographies and Checklists, 41. London: Grant and Cutler, 1983.

Whitbourn, Christine J. *The "Arcipreste de Talavera" and the Literature of Love*. Occasional Papers in Modern Languages, 7. Hull: University, 1970.

Young, Howard T. *The Victorious Expression: A Study of Four Contemporary Spanish Poets—Miguel de Unamuno, Antonio Machado, Juan Ramón Jiménez, Federico García Lorca*. Madison: The University of Wisconsin Press, 1966.

Zumthor, Paul. "Narrative and Anti-Narrative: *Le Roman de la Rose*." Trans. Frank Yeomans. *YFS*, 51 (1974), 185-204.